学校的样子

WHAT THE SCHOOL LOOKS LIKE

镜头里的北京十一学校

Beijing National Day School Through The Lens

李强／著

Li Qiang

五洲传播出版社
China Intercontinental Press

图书在版编目（CIP）数据

学校的样子：汉英对照 / 李强著；李航译 . -- 北京：五洲传播出版社，2022.9

ISBN 978-7-5085-4851-7

Ⅰ . ①学… Ⅱ . ①李… ②李… Ⅲ . ①北京十一学校－图集 Ⅳ . ① G639.281-64

中国版本图书馆 CIP 数据核字 (2022) 第 147422 号

作　　者	李　强	
翻　　译	李　航	
出 版 人	关　宏	
责任编辑	梁　媛	
选题策划	源创图书	
装帧设计	红方众文　张芳芳　龚　爽	
出版发行	五洲传播出版社	
地　　址	北京市海淀区北三环中路 31 号生产力大楼 B 座 6 层	
邮　　编	100088	
发行电话	010-82005927，010-82007837	
网　　址	http://www.cicc.org.cn，http://www.thatsbooks.com	
印　　刷	北京中石油彩色印刷有限责任公司	
版　　次	2022 年 9 月第 1 版第 1 次印刷	
开　　本	889mm×1194mm　1/16	
字　　数	120 千	
定　　价	98.00 元	

序

很喜欢李强老师这本书的名字。展现一所学校的样子，是很难的一件事情，尤其是以图片的方式展现，更是难上加难。李强老师用十年的时间，游走在绿树红楼之间，以他的热忱、勤奋、敏锐和坚守，给我们带来的这本《学校的样子》，让我们为之一振，虽所见皆是熟悉的场景，却仍然感觉耳目一新。

学校的样子本该就是孩子们的样子。学校因为学生而存在，教师因为学生而相聚。衡量一所学校存在的价值，当然应该以它育人的成果作为标准。然而，教育的成果却并非仅体现在学生毕业的时刻，更不仅仅是考试的分数，大部分成果需要十年、二十年、三十年甚或更长的时间才可以显现。世俗往往缺乏这样的耐心。即使长期在校园里的人们，也常常茫然无知。于是，或者急功近利，仅仅追求眼前的分数；或者信念缺失，找不到自己的职业价值。李强老师通过《学校的样子》，把教师的职业价值定格，以图片呈现的瞬间让我们发现那些熟视无睹的细节、置若罔闻的笑声、屡见不鲜的新奇。这个过程其实是还原了教育的本义。教育的价值是发生在过程之中的。有了好的过程，我们完全可以自信地说，只问耕耘，不问收获。因为这种良好的校园生态，往往就是孩子们未来成长的养料。从这个意义上说，李强的这本《学校的样子》帮了我们教育者一个大忙，让我们可以预知孩子们未来的样子。

长期以来，我们校园里的摄影镜头患上了学生遗忘症，它们聚焦的大都是领导视察或各种活动的群体现场。尤其让我们抱憾的是，即使去一些所谓声名远扬的学校考察学习，校方也总是让你去那些见不到学生的"高大上"的地方：或者富丽的场馆，或者校园里的湖桥和雕塑，或者贴有院士校友照片的名人橱窗。说实话，见不到在校学习的学生，让我们判定并学习这所学校的价值追求或者教育风格，实在是心孤意怯。我很欣赏李强老师在校园里的样子，满眼盯着学生，满脸写着学生，满嘴叨念着学生。一个满心全是学生的老师，才可能是孩子们喜爱的样子，而这个样子，其实是十一学校老师的最为可敬的形象。

李强老师在大学里学的是政治专业，后来，因为学校要设置一个特长教育办公室，于是就请爱好摄影并带着一个学生摄影社团的他改行做了这个办公室的主任。那一年是 1995 年，我刚好调任山东高密一中校长。那时的我颇有点担心，担心这样一个决定会影响到一位优秀老师的专业发展。后来的事实反而证明了当时决策的"英明"。当然，这样的"英明"完全是由李强老师自己证明的，他后来也曾到北京电影学院专修摄影。不过，这同时也给我们这些做教育的人一个启发：人的天赋和潜能真的需要发现和挖掘。

我愿意向各位同行推荐这本书，请不要把它误以为是一本摄影图片集，它只是以图片的方式，帮助我们切入教育之中。它以独特的方式为我们提供更加鲜活的画面，给我们更多想像的空间和再创造的可能，带我们走进一个教育的艺术世界。

想念图片中和没在图片中的那些孩子们，我在每一届的毕业典礼上都会说的一句话，今天还要再说一遍：祝你们一生幸福。

李希贵

2022 年 7 月 28 日

（李希贵，中国教育学会副会长、北京第一实验学校校长、北京十一学校原校长。）

Preface

I really like the title of this book. It is difficult to show what a school looks like, especially if it is only shown in pictures. Mr. Li Qiang has spent ten years walking among the green trees and red buildings on campus. With his enthusiasm, diligence, keenness and perseverance, he brought us this wonderful book named "What a School Looks Like". Through this book, the familiar scenes on campus bring us a refreshing feeling.

Schools are supposed to reflect what kids look like, as schools exist because of kids, and teachers meet because of them too. To measure the value of a school's existence, of course, it should be based on the results of her education. However, the results of education are not shown at the moment when students graduate, nor simply shown through test scores. Most of the results appear after ten, twenty, thirty years or even longer. The world often lacks such patience. Even people who have been on campus for a long time are often ignorant: they are either eager for quick success, pursuing immediate test scores, or lack of belief, unable to find their professional value. Mr. Li Qiang captured the professional value of teachers through *What the School Looks Like*. The moments presented in pictures let us discover the details that we have turned a blind eye to, the laughter that has fallen on deaf ears, and the novelties that are often seen but neglected. This process actually restores the original meaning of education: the value of education occurs in the process. With a good process, we can confidently say that we only care about the cultivation, not the harvest. A good campus ecology is often the nourishment for children's future growth. In this sense, this book has done us educators a big favor, allowing us to predict what our children will look like in the future.

For a long time, the camera lenses on our campus have forgotten students—— most of them focus on the scene of administrators' inspections or various group activities. What we especially regret is that even if you visit the so-called prestigious schools, people always lead you to fancy places where you can't see students: grand venues, delicate bridges and sculptures, or windows with photos of famous alumni. To be honest, if we can't see students on campus, hardly can we evaluate or appreciate the educational style and value of the school. I admire how Mr. Li looks like on campus. He is looking at students, talking about students, and thinking of students at any time. A teacher whose heart is filled with students will certainly be favored by students, and such a teacher represents the most respectable image of educators at BNDS.

Mr. Li Qiang majored in politics in college. When I was the Principal of Gaomi No. 1 High School of Shandong Province in 1995, I invited Mr. Li Qiang, who loved photography and led a student photography club, to be the director of a newly established Special Education Office. I was quite worried at that time, afraid that such a decision would affect the professional development of a teacher. Later facts proved how "brilliant" this decision was. Of course, such "brilliance" was completely proved by Mr. Li Qiang himself, who later went to Beijing Film Academy for further study in photography. However, this also inspires educators: people's talents and potential really need to be discovered and tapped.

I would like to recommend this book to all teachers and educators. Please don't mistake it for a photographic collection. It uses pictures to help us reach into education. It provides us with a more vivid picture of education in a unique way, gives us more space for imagination and possibility of re-creation, and takes us into an artistic world of education.

I miss the kids who are shown in the picture and those who are not. I'd like to send my best wishes one more time to all my dear students. As what I said at the graduation ceremony every year: I wish you happiness all your life!

Li Xigui

July 28, 2022

(Li Xigui, Vice President of the Chinese Society of Education, Principal of Beijing No.1 Experimental School, Former Principal of Beijing National Day School.)

前　言

　　有一所学校，以国庆之日命名，与共和国一起成长，以民族精神培育人；有一所学校，以创造适合每一位学生发展的教育为使命，促使人形成健全的人格，提高人文素养；有一所学校，海纳百川，包容共生，聚天下英才，做创新事业，以一流的质量和卓越的队伍为目标。这所学校，着力于培养志存高远、诚信笃行、思想活跃、言行规范的民族脊梁和社会栋梁；这所学校，是一所不一样的学校，这就是我眼中的北京十一学校！

　　近些年来，北京十一学校在教育教学领域进行了根本性变革，带来了整个学校的转型，尤其是在课程体系方面，充分尊重学生的选择，实行选课走班，创造适合每一位学生发展的教育。十一学校有着丰富多彩的创新性较强的活动，形成了独特的文化氛围，引起了社会的广泛关注。2014年2月27日，教育部把新闻发布会现场搬到一所中学——北京十一学校，专门推荐这所中学的改革经验，这是前所未有的。

　　这是一所与众不同的学校：这里是一个充满选择的校园，以学生为主体，把选择权交给学生；在学科教学上，从学生的需求出发，开发独特的课程体系；没有传统意义上的行政班，没有班主任，每个学生的课程表都不一样，学生们每天根据自己的选择在不同教室走班上课；校园里大大小小的活动都由学生来承办，有各种各样的学生社团等；这里的学生阳光、自信、快乐，每个学生的脸上都有幸福的笑容，而且高考成绩也名列北京市前茅。

　　镜中写春秋，方寸汇风云。为了追求摄影之美，过去的二十多年我利用节假日带着相机去了许多地方。大自然的奇美瑰丽、各地习俗的丰富多彩，为我提供了无穷的创作源泉。近年来，我在从事摄影教学之余，拍摄比较多的是校园生活。与风光摄影相比，校园摄影更侧重表现人物活动，并且要体现一些教育理念。在校园内拍摄，需要融入校园生活，通过抓拍的方式去捕捉细节，表现一些生动而又感人的瞬间。

在过去的十年时间，我认真观察十一学校的变革，透过镜头记录学校的变化，为基础教育改革留下真实的瞬间，也希望通过一本书来呈现这所学校的形态。为此，我选择内涵丰富并具有较强感染力的图片汇编成册，希望通过这些图片来展示学校不同领域的变化，折射学校的价值文化体系，并从不同侧面展现十一学校的创新做法和卓越魅力。

在这本书里，关于这所学校的独特之处，我运用关键词和关键点来梳理影像背后的信息主线。本书用了八个部分来分别表述"快乐、充满选择、平等、自由呼吸、寻找同伴、学生做主、注重体验和国际化"这些关键词；为了让读者准确理解这八个关键词，每章开篇引用了体现十一学校办学理念的概括性文字，并归纳了一些关键点，再对每个关键点进行了简要阐述。全书大约涵盖 58 个关键点。这样便于大家全面、系统而又直观地认识十一学校，发现不一样的十一学校。

十一学校有一批具有教育家情怀和境界的教职工，有大量富有个性、创意而又积极进取的学生，每天都有许多值得拍摄的活动，有许多让人感动的教育故事。我经常是跑着去拍摄，用感动按下相机快门，这或许正是十一学校的教育感召力，令我们一直在奋勇前行！

我是在十一学校 60 年校庆前开始拍摄这所学校的，而今年国庆节将是十一学校建校 70 周年的日子，在过去的十年里十一学校的改革不断走向深入，学校也发生了很大的变化，我的相机也留下了许多值得回味的瞬间，谨以此书向十一学校的 70 华诞献礼！

Foreword

There is a school named after the National Day of the People's Republic of China, growing with the country and nurturing students with a noble national spirit; there is a school that takes establishing educational mode suitable for every students' development as its mission; there is a school that embraces all diversities, gathering talents from all over the world to promote high quality educational innovation. It is a school that strives to cultivating social pillars and national backbones with ambitions, integrity, creativity, and discipline. This is Beijing National Day School in my eyes–a unique and great school!

In recent years, Beijing National Day School (BNDS) has made fundamental changes in the field of education, bringing about a transformation of the entire school. The transformed curriculum system and course selection system fully respects students' choices and establish an education mode that suits the development of every individual. BNDS has a rich series of innovative activities which form a unique cultural atmosphere, attracting widespread attention from the society. On February 27, 2014, China's Ministry of Education held an unprecedented press conference at BNDS, specifically for recommending the reform of the school.

This is a unique school. It is a campus full of independent choices, where students are the main focus and are given the right to choose. In subject teaching, a unique curriculum is designed to meet diverse needs of students. There is neither administrative class nor headmaster in the traditional sense, and each student attends classes in different classrooms every day following their individualized timetable. Various campus activities and student clubs are all run by students. Walking into BNDS, you will find energetic, confident and joyful students everywhere. Every student wears a beaming smile, and their high school entrance exam results are among the top in Beijing.

The wind and clouds in spring and autumn are all written on my camera lens. In order to pursue the beauty of photography, I took my camera to many places during my free time in the past two decades. The beauty of nature and the richness of local customs provided me with endless sources of creativity. In recent years, in addition to work in teaching photography, I shot more of campus life. Compared with landscape photography, campus photography is more colorful as it focuses on people's activities and reflects education philosophies. To shoot on campus, I need to integrate into campus life, capture some details through snapshots, thus showing more vivid and touching moments.

Over the past ten years, I've carefully observed the transformation of BNDS and recorded the changes through my lens. I wish to collect real moments of basic education reform and present unique features of the school in this book. For this purpose, I compiled images with rich connotation and strong impacts to display changes in different aspects of the school, reflect the value and culture of the school, and present the innovative practices and excellent glamour of BNDS from various angles.

In this book, I use key words and points to sort out main lines of information behind the images, through which unique features of the school are revealed. The book illustrates eight key points in eight chapters: joy, choices, equality, independent learning, companionship, student-led, experience-based, and internationalization. To give readers an accurate understanding of these concepts, I quote at the beginning of each chapter from introductions to BNDS school philosophy. With each chapter introducing and illustrating several key points, the book covers approximately 57 key points so as to make it easy for readers to understand BNDS in a direct, comprehensive and systematic way. Through this book, readers are able to discover more about BNDS that are invisible to the eye.

At BNDS there are teaching staff with sentiments of real educators, and students with rich personalities, creativity and motivation. There are many activities and touching educational stories worth being recorded every day. I often run to shoot, and click the camera shutter while being moved. This is perhaps the educational inspiration brought by BNDS, which keeps us moving forward.

I started photographing this school before its 60th anniversary, and this year on October 1st marks the 70th anniversary of BNDS. Along with the constant deepening of educational reform in the past decade, the school has undergone great changes, and my camera has also recorded many memorable moments. I would like to dedicate this book to the 70th birthday of Beijing National Day School!

Content
目录

01

——

快乐的学校
A School Full of Joy

◆ 最好的教育应该是着眼于孩子一生发展的教育，应该是关注孩子心灵的教育，应该是使师生感受到自由、幸福和快乐的教育。

◆ 优质学校主要是从学校外部人们的感受来定位，而理想学校则更多的是要遵从学生和老师的感受，他们是否感到愉悦和幸福来定位。

◆ 一个孩子的成长如果始终在绷紧的套子里挣扎，他就不会有健康的翅膀，许多时候，他们需要放松，他们需要属于自己的天空，如果我们能够有一些时间闭上紧盯着他们的眼睛，给他们一些自由，回报我们的也许正是我们希望看到的他们的自律和自主。

◆ 有人说，评价一所学校可以有很简单的方法，看一看校园里学生们的眼神也就可以判断学校的优劣。尽管我们知道这是一个很有道理却不便操作的方法，但其中包含的价值取向却是大家普遍认同的，我们理应把评价学校的着眼点、落脚点和着力点转到学生身上。

◆ 我们不仅要着力于孩子们未来的幸福，他们现时的幸福也理应成为我们共同的关注点。如果是这样的话，我们完全有理由去全力打造学生向往的理想学校，尽管走向这样的理想学校要经历许许多多艰难与风险，包括经营者心灵的磨难，但是，这个追求是崇高的、值得的。

◆ The best education should focus on children's lifelong development, should pay attention to children's heart and soul, and should enable teachers and students to feel freedom, joy and happiness.

◆ A high-quality school is mainly positioned by the feelings of people outside the school, while an ideal school should most importantly follow feelings of students and teachers inside, caring about their joy and happiness.

◆ A child will not have healthy wings if he grows up struggling in a tight cage. Most of the time, children need to relax and enjoy their own sky. If sometimes we close our eyes that keep staring at them and give them more freedom, in return for, as what we hope to see, their self-discipline and self-motivation.

◆ People say that there is a very simple way to evaluate a good school, which is to look at the eyes of students on campus. This method is reasonable but unpractical, yet the value behind it is generally recognized by everyone: while evaluating a school, we ought to transfer our focus, goals and strength to the students on campus.

◆ We should not only focus on our children's future well-being, but also their present well-being. In this case, we have every reason to spare no effort to build an ideal school that students yearn for. Although the path to such a school will be full of trials and tribulations, including operators' mental ordeal, this pursuit will be noble and worthwhile.

富有创新性的开学典礼
Innovative School Opening Ceremony

　　大部分学校的开学典礼通常是以开大会的形式举行，内容往往是采取学校领导讲话、教师和学生代表发言。而十一学校的开学典礼却是活泼多样的，注重学生的参与感，充满惊喜和对新学年的憧憬。开学典礼主要是由学生团队来策划筹办，每年的内容和形式都不一样。富有创新性是开学典礼的一大特点，所以每年广大师生对开学典礼都充满了期待，就像期待新学年的到来一样。

　　Most of the school opening ceremony is usually a general meeting, including speeches by school leaders, teachers and student representatives. But at BNDS it is more lively with various activities. The ceremony with lots of surprises carries best wishes for the new school year and allows students to fully engage. The school opening ceremony of BNDS is mainly planned and organized by student teams, and the content and form of the ceremony varied every year. As innovation is a major feature of this event, teachers and students are full of expectations for the ceremony as well as for the arrival of the new school year.

参加马术课的学生骑马参加开学典礼（2013.09.01）

Students from the equestrianism class riding horses at the school opening ceremony

开学典礼上跳舞的同学们（2014.08.31）

Students dancing at the school opening ceremony

W学 校 的 样 子
HAT THE SCHOOL LOOKS LIKE

手持开学护照的同学们（2020.09.01）

Students holding the school opening passport

欢乐的泼水节
Joyful Water Splashing Festival

　　每年夏天放暑假前夕，十一学校大操场上都会水光跃溅，笑声飞扬，分年级的泼水节已成为这里独特的风俗。学校会事先在操场晒几池水，师生们在简短的仪式后就迫不及待地泼了起来。背景音乐热烈激昂，五颜六色的水盆、水桶纷纷登场，老师学生难分彼此，共同嬉戏，泼得酣畅淋漓，玩得不亦乐乎，水声、笑声、欢呼声共同交织成激情四射的乐章。泼水节不仅让学生和老师得以放松，也拉近了师生间的距离，留下了属于每个学生的美好中学回忆。

　　Every year before the summer vacation, the stadium at BNDS will be splashed with water and laughter—the Water Splashing Festival has become a unique custom here. The school will prepare a few pools of water beforehand. After a brief ceremony, teachers and students can't wait to splash water on one another. With the exciting background music and colorful basins in hands, teachers and students play together, and have a lot of fun. The sound of water, laughter and cheers are intertwined into a passionate symphony. The Water Splashing Festival not only allows students and teachers to relax, but also shortens the distance between them, leaving a good memory for each student in high school.

参加泼水节的师生（2015.06.30）

Students and teachers at the Water Splashing Festival

泼水节总是在欢声笑语中度过（2017.07.11）

The Water Splashing Festival is always full of laughter

激情四溢的狂欢节
Passionate School Carnival

　　每年最后一天学校会举行狂欢节，全校师生倾情参与，在参与中分享快乐，在分享中建立融洽的师生关系，共同迎接新年的到来。学校大操场是狂欢节的主场地，各功能楼也会举办不同特色的小型活动。每年狂欢节校长会按学生的意愿进行装扮，已被学生安排扮演的角色就有"加勒比海盗船长"、"魔法学院的邓布利多校长"和"变形金刚大黄蜂"等，老师们也会装扮成各种卡通形象。狂欢节营造了一个激情四溢的校园狂欢氛围，也成为十一校园最隆重的活动之一。

　　On the last day of each year, the school will hold a carnival to welcome the new year. Teachers and students of the whole school participate enthusiastically and establish a harmonious relationship while sharing happiness with each other. The school stadium is the main venue for the carnival, and some special activities will be held in other school buildings. Every year the principal will dress up according to students' wish. The roles that have been chosen for the principal include "Pirate of the Caribbean", "Professor Dumbledore" from "Hogwards School of Witchcraft and Wizardry", and "Bumblebee". Teachers will also dress up as various cartoon characters. The carnival creates a passionate campus atmosphere and becomes one of the most grand events at BNDS.

狂欢节巡游小火车 (2012.12.29)

Carnival parade train

不同装扮的同学们（2013.12.31）

Students in different costumes

W学 校 的 样 子
HAT THE SCHOOL LOOKS LIKE

每年不同的装扮（2012.12.29）

Different costumes for the principal

狂欢节上校长的角色扮演（2019.12.31）

Cosplay of the principal at the carnival

狂欢节上笑容灿烂的同学们（2019.12.31）

Students with bright smiles on the carnival

每年狂欢节都有不同的主题（2019.12.31）

Diverse theme of the carnival each year

人人参与的体育季
Sports Season Open to Everyone

　　十一学校改变了传统运动会少数人比赛、多数人观看的局面，举行形式灵活多样、人人参与的体育季。体育季比赛的内容就像体育课一样丰富多彩，并且有许多趣味性、创新性的活动，许多创意都来自学生。有时，体育季还会邀请一些体育方面的世界冠军或者球星与学生们互动，更增加了体育季的吸引力。

　　BNDS has changed the pattern of tradition sports events in which only a few people can participate while most people watch. The Sports Season with flexible and diverse activities is open to everyone at BNDS. The activities are as colorful as PE classes, and more interesting and innovative activities are designed by students. Sometimes world champions and famous athletes are invited to interact with students, which enhance the appeal of the Sports Season.

WHAT THE SCHOOL LOOKS LIKE 学 校 的 样 子

胜利在望（2019.10.11）

Victory in sight

施展才华的艺术节
Art Festival to Showcase Talents

　　许多学校都举办艺术节，但十一学校的艺术节完全由学生承办，前期策划、节目确定、设施设备等都由学生完成，并且每年的特色都不一样，学校团委只是作为主办单位负责招标，学生会在其中发挥比较大的作用。艺术节为学生搭建了自我锻造和施展才华的舞台，多彩的活动丰富了校园文化生活。

　　Art Festival at BNDS is completely held by students. Their jobs include preliminary event planning, program design, equipment preparation and so forth. The themes and features are different every year. The Student Union plays a major role in holding the event, while the School Youth League Committee only helps to invite bids. The Art Festival builds up a platform for students to practice and display their talents, and colorful activities enrich the cultural life on campus.

舞动的旋律（2017.11.10）

Dancing melody

演出之后的笑容 （2019.04.18）

Smiles after the performance

不唯高考，赢得高考

Winning the College Entrance Exam without Exclusively Focusing on It

　　不唯高考却赢得高考，十一学校近些年高考高分人数位居北京市前列。学生多元、个性发展的特点得以进一步彰显。提高升学率不是目的，全面提高人的素质、促进学生积极主动发展才是十一学校孜孜以求的目标。十一学校对所有学生实行学分管理，每一位学生不仅要在专业领域，还要在体育与艺术技能、综合实践活动、社团活动等方面获得足够学分才能毕业。

　　In recent years, BNDS has ranked among the top in Beijing in the number of high score students in college entrance examination, but BNDS never focuses on improving the rate of college admission, but on improving the quality of students and promoting their positive and active development. The school adopts credit system for all students. Before graduation, each student must achieve required credits not only in academic fields, but also in sports and art, club activities, and comprehensive practical activities.

高考前一天，老师和同学们玩起了掰手腕的游戏。(2012.06.06)

The day before the college entrance exam,
a teacher played the game of arm wrestling with students

高三同学户外拓展活动（2018.07.12）

The outdoor expansion activities of grade 12 students

为参加高考的同学点赞加油（2021.06.07）

Cheering for the students who took the college entrance examination

02

充满选择的学校

A School Providing Many Choices

◆ 教育永远不可能让孩子们在同一个舞台上都光彩照人，也不可能以同样的机会让不一样的孩子赢得同样的成功，我们具有竞争优势的方式只有一个，就是造就一个充满选择的校园。

◆ 选择常常是和责任连在一起的，当孩子有了自主选择的权利的时候，他才会全力以赴，他才能披荆斩棘。在选择中学会选择，在选择中规划人生。

◆ 学科教室的建设，完全按照学科学习的需要配置资源，依据学科学习的规律装点环境，努力创造条件，让学生能够手脑并用，听说并重，当用枪时用枪，当使棍时使棍，学习生态自然平衡而和谐。

◆ 学校刚刚开设选修课的时候，大部分学生凭兴趣去选择是可以理解的，但我们开设选修课的目的绝不仅仅是为了满足学生的兴趣，这只是一个课程的初始目标。选修课应该和学生未来的生活、未来的成长，和学生对未来职业的选择及学生未来的人生规划联系在一起。

◆ 从一个角度看学生，可能只有百分之一的天才；从多个角度看学生，也许就有百分之九十九的天才。多一把衡量的尺子，也就增加了成才的可能。

◆ 教育的重要使命应该是发现，发现每个学生不同的特点与个性，创造多元的产品来满足学生的不同需求。教育工作者应该通过不一样的课程，把看上去差不多的孩子变得越来越像他们自己。因为未来属于有不同特质的孩子。

- Education can never make all children shine on the same stage, nor can different children win the same success with the same opportunities. There is only one way for a school to gain competitive advantage, which is to create a campus enviornment full of choices.

- Choice is often related to responsibility. When children have the right to choose independently, they will go all out and overcome obstacles. They will learn to make better choices, and plan their life better.

- The classrooms are built in accordance with the needs of subject learning. The environment is decorated according to the rules of subject learning. We create conditions for students to use both hands and brains, to listen and talk, and to choose appropriate learning tools as they need. The ecology of learning is natural, balanced and harmonious.

- When the school started providing elective courses, most students choose courses based on their interests, which is understandable, but the purpose of our elective courses is more than satisfying students' interests. Elective courses should be connected to students' future life and growth, and their career choices and life plans.

- If you look at students from one angle, you may only see 1% talents; but if you look at them from many angles, you may see 99% talents. Multi-angle evaluation also increases students' possibility of becoming talents.

- The important mission of education is to discover. Discover different characteristics and personalities of each student, and create diverse products to meet their different needs. Educators should make similar students become more like themselves through different courses, because the future belongs to children with different traits.

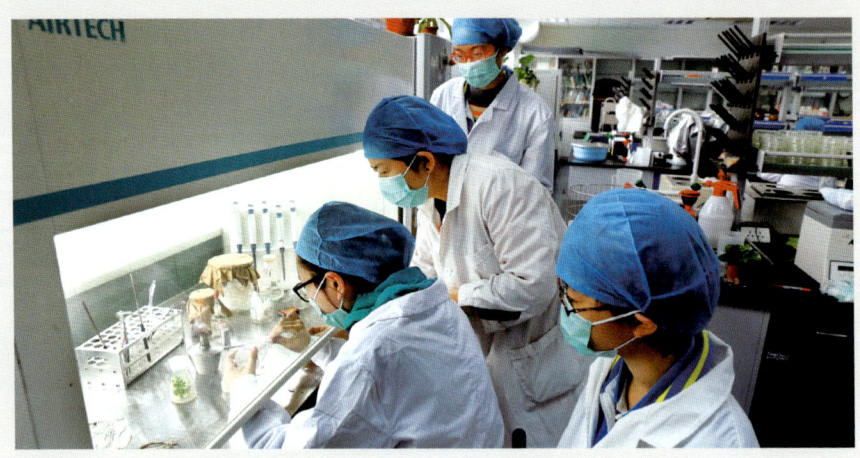

多元的课程体系
Diverse Curriculum System

　　课程是学校改革的核心，只有改变课程才会使学校发生根本性的变化。十一学校全面推动课程改革，使传统的所有学生读相同的书、上相同的课的单一模式发生了根本改变，建立起了"分层、分类、综合、特需"的课程体系。学校的课程分成了不同的门类系列，并且大部分是面向学生个体可自由选择的课程。在十一学校，学生可以根据自己的实际情况选择自己需要的课程，每一个学生都有属于自己的独一无二的课程表，使得自由个性、素质的培养成为可能。

　　Curriculum lies in the core of school reform. Only by changing the curriculum will the school realize fundamental changes. BNDS promotes all-round curriculum reform and changes the traditional education mode in which all students read the same books and take the same classes. A new curriculum system is built up including "layered courses, classified courses, comprehensive courses, and courses for special needs". The courses are divided into different categories, and most of them can be chosen by students freely. As students can choose different courses according to their personal situation, each student will have a unique timetable. In this way, the school makes it possible to cultivate free personalities and qualities.

选择不同线路的游学类课程（2014.11.15）

Different lines chosen by students in studying tour courses

选择适合自己的课程进行学习（2017.12.25）

Choose courses that suit every individual

技术课程成果交流展示活动（2019.05.26）

Technical course results exchange and display activities

具有各自学科特点的学科教室

Classrooms with Distinctive Subject Characteristics

　　把传统的行政班转变为教学班后，十一学校的教室发生了很大的改变，承载了更多的教育功能。一方面，从单一的上课功能转变为上课、读书、实验、讨论、教研等多种功能；另一方面，从一样的教室转变为具有不同学科特点的学科教室。一花，一草，一书屋；一师，一友，一学堂。在整个变革的过程中，各个科目的图书、仪器等学习资源进入教室，老师也被分配到自己负责的学科教室，将办公桌搬进教室，增加了与学生交流的机会，也为学生的自主学习提供了便利。

　　After the traditional administrative classes were transformed into teaching classes, classrooms at BNDS have undergone great changes, carrying more educational functions. On one hand, classrooms have changed from a single function of having class to multiple functions, such as reading, experiment, discussion, and teaching research; on the other hand, they have changed from the same look to varied looks displaying distinctive subject characteristics. During the whole reform process, books, instruments and other subject learning resources were brought into respective classrooms. Teachers moved their desks into subject classrooms, which increases communication with students and facilitates students' independent learning.

生物教室内的蜥蜴（2014.11.19）

Lizards in the biology classroom

具有功能分区的摄影教室（2014.12.12）

Photography classroom with functional partitions

随时可以进行实验的化学教室（2015.01.13）

Chemistry classroom ready for experiments at any time

教室内课桌的不同排列组合（2018.12.05）

Different arrangement and combination of desks in the classroom

同学在动漫教室学习创作（2021.12.26）

Students learn to create in the animation classroom

生机盎然的生物教室（2021.12.31）

Lively biology classroom

个性化的选课走班
Personalized Course Selection System

　　在分类分层的课程体系下，原有的行政班级管理模式被打破，学校实施走班选课制。学生既要选择适合自己的课程模块，又要选择适合自己的学习时段。通过选课，每个学生都形成了一张个性化的课表，按照自己的课表，到不同的学科教室上课，在不同的教学班之间流动，老师们则在各自固定的教室里等待学生上课。在选课走班的体制下，学生更灵活自主地规划自己的学习内容与学习时间，真正成为自己学业的主人，为自己的个性化发展掌舵。

Under the classified and layered curriculum system, the original administrative class management model was broken, and the school implemented the optional class system. Students need to choose both the course modules and the study periods that suit them. Through course selection, each student produces a personalized timetable. Following their own timetable, students go to different subject classrooms and switch between different teaching classes, while teachers wait for students in their fixed subject classrooms. Under this system, students can plan their own learning content and learning time more flexibly and independently, and truly become the masters of their own studies, steering their own personalized development.

教学楼走廊内，每个同学都有一个储物柜。(2014.05.14)

Each student has a cabinet in the corridor of the teaching building

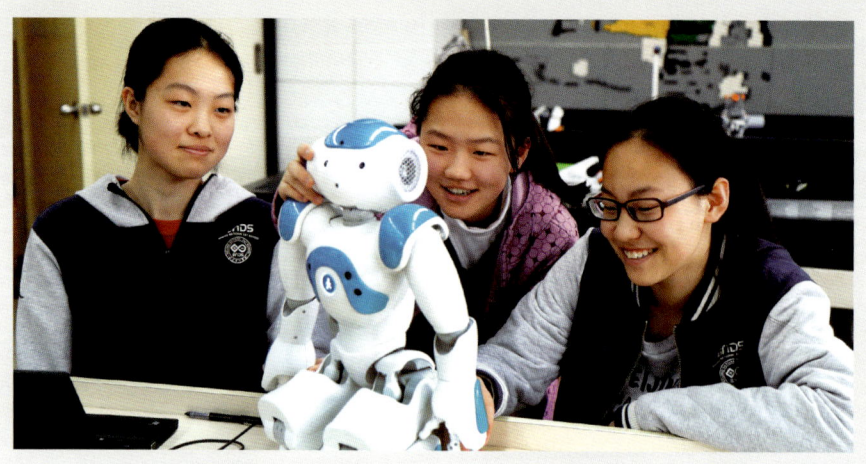

与职业倾向结合的技术课程
Technical Courses Combined with Career Orientation

为了开阔学生的视野，将现在的学习与将来的职业倾向结合起来，学校设置了机械技术、机器人技术、影视技术、汽车造型设计、服装设计与制作、计算机科学、人工智能、航模、电子技术等 19 个模块的分类技术课程，并配备了相应的教学设备和专业教师，在开课时间、场所等方面给予充分保证。亲自动手，亲身实践，不仅满足了学生的兴趣需要，同时又提高了学生的技术素养和实践水平，培养了学生的创新能力。

In order to broaden students' horizons and combine their current learning with future career orientation, BNDS has set up 19 modules of technical courses including mechanical technology, robotics, film and television technology, automotive design, clothing design and production, computer science, artificial intelligence, model aircraft, electronic technology and so on. The courses are equipped with corresponding teaching equipment and professional teachers, and the class time and spaces are fully guaranteed by the school . Students can gain authentic experience only through hands-on practice. The courses not only meet the needs of students' interests, but also improve their technical literacy and practical abilities, and cultivate their innovation.

机械技术实验室（2015.01.30）

Mechanical technology lab

外国友人在技术教室参观（2019.05.18）

Foreign guests visiting the technical classroom

可获得学分的学生影院
Student Cinema with Credits

　　在十一学校，看电影也是一门课程，学生在学校影院看电影，可以获得一定的学分。学校影院播放的电影都是根据学生的意见选择的，影院的经理由学生担任，海报设计、观后感征集等都由学生来操作。当然，每次电影课程都有相应的指导老师进行点评。电影通过艺术的手法表现他人的人生故事。看电影既是感受艺术的过程，也是丰富阅历的课程。经典影视作品富有育人价值，是一项关乎于人生的课程。

　　Watching movies has also been designed as a course at BNDS, in which students can get certain credits by watching movies at the school cinema. The movies played at the cinema are selected according to students' opinions. The cinema is managed by students, and they also design posters and collect film reviews. Of course, each movie class is guided by an instructor. Movies express life stories of others through artistic means, so watching movies is not only a process of experiencing art, but also a course to enrich experience. Good movies teach students lessons about life.

同学们在学校影院观看电影（2017.12.11）

Students watching a movie at the school cinema

开设多语种课程
Multi-Language Courses

　　为了让学生有机会了解不同国家和民族的文化，学校开设了法语、德语、日语、西班牙语、俄语等小语种课程，使语言课程的内容由原来单一的英语向多种外语和少数民族语言延伸，未来的世界公民将从这里启航。

　　In order to provide suitable courses for students studying abroad, and give students opportunities to understand cultures of different countries and nationalities, BNDS offers French, German, Japanese, Spanish, Russian and other language courses. Language courses has been expanded from the only English course to multilingual and minority language courses, preparing students for the future world.

参加多语种课学习的同学们（2021.12.23）

Students attending a multi-language class

具有综合育人价值的艺术课程
Art Courses For All-round Development

　　为培养兴趣、陶冶情操、发展特长，增强学生的合作、交往等能力，学校将传统的音乐、美术课整合为艺术类课程，并具体分为中国画、油画、版画、书法、造型基础、摄影、动漫、视觉传达设计、影视编导与制作、音乐基础、戏剧等模块。学生们有机会成为导演、编剧、演员，倾尽心血铸成自己的代表作。此外，学校还组建了多个专业艺术团队，如：金帆交响乐团、金帆民乐团、金帆合唱团、舞蹈团等，给热爱艺术的学生搭建了施展才华的广阔舞台。

　　In order to cultivate students' interests, edify their sentiments, develop talents, and enhance their abilities of cooperation and communication, BNDS integrates traditional music and fine art courses into art courses, which are specifically divided into Chinese painting, oil painting, printmaking, calligraphy, modeling basics, photography, animation design, visual communication design, film and television choreography and production, music foundation, drama, etc. Students have the opportunity to become directors, screenwriters and actors, and put all their efforts into casting their own masterpieces. In addition, the school has also established a number of professional art groups, which includes the Golden Sail Symphony Orchestra, Folk Orchestra, the Golden Sail Choir, Dance Troupe, etc. A broad platform is provided for art lovers to display their talents.

专业戏剧课展演（2015.12.24）

Showcase of professional drama class

舞蹈课期末演出（2021.06.18）

Final performance of dance class

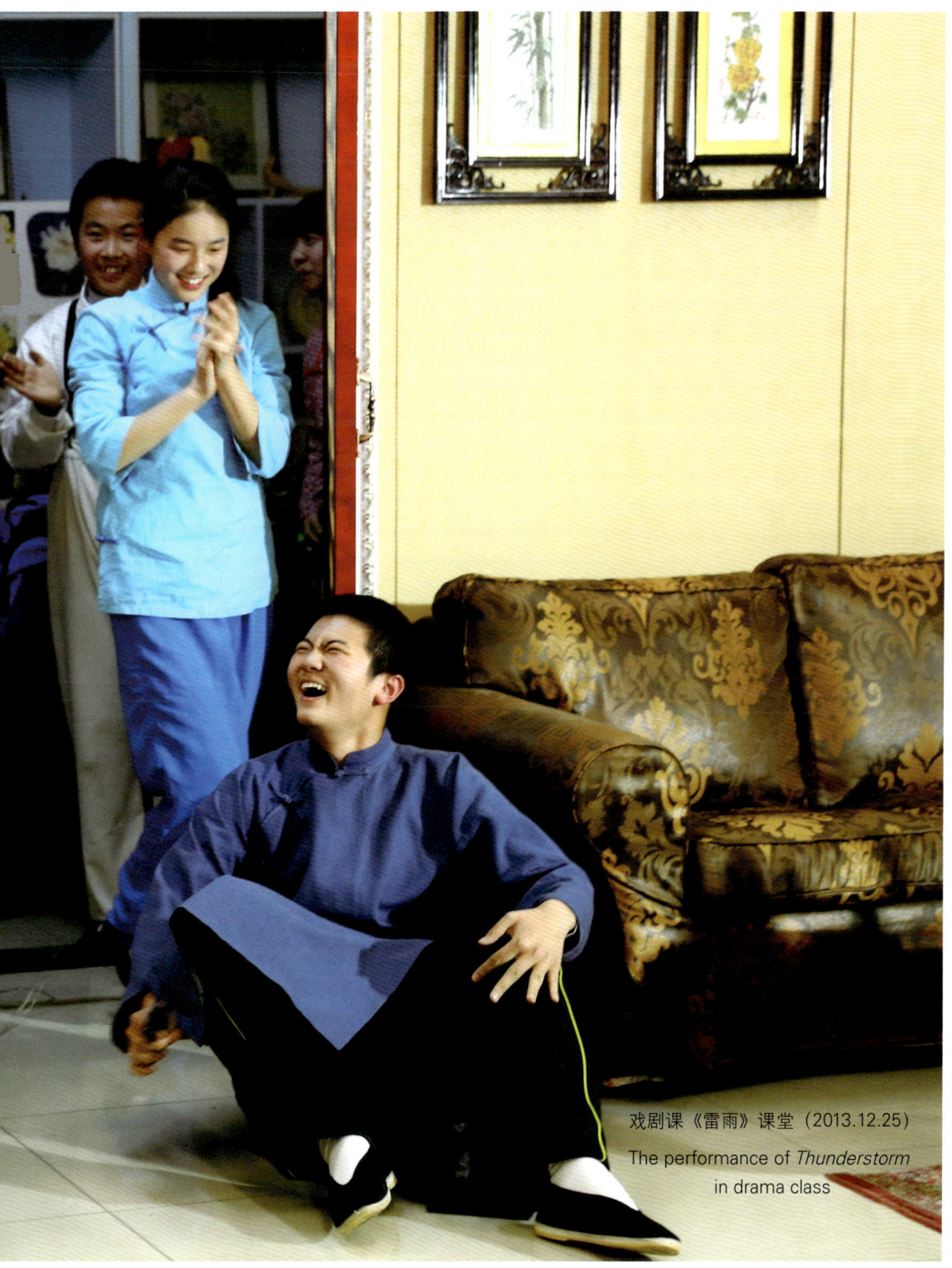

戏剧课《雷雨》课堂（2013.12.25）
The performance of *Thunderstorm* in drama class

多样的体育课程模块
Diverse Physical Education Courses

　　原来单调统一的体育课被田径、篮球、足球、排球、网球、棒球、垒球、橄榄球、游泳、马术、滑雪、击剑、独轮车、攀岩等二十多种丰富多彩的课程替代，学生可以根据自己的兴趣进行选择，以最大限度地满足学生的运动兴趣和身体锻炼的需要，使他们在体育课中锻炼品格，培养坚韧不拔的精神。

　　The former monotonous PE classes have been replaced by more than 20 colorful courses for students to choose, such as track and field, basketball, football, volleyball, tennis, baseball, softball, rugby, swimming, horse riding, skiing, fencing, unicycle, rock climbing, etc. The courses meet students' different sports interests and physical exercise needs to the greatest extent. PE classes help students to be devoted, perseverant, and resilient.

射箭课（2015.06.04）

Archery class

激发潜能的校园机会榜

Campus Opportunity List for Unleashing Potential

学校尽可能扩大学生自主成长的空间，通过"校园机会榜"把适于学生的事务，以公开竞标的方式选择承办者。国际文化日、毕业典礼、成人仪式、升旗仪式、名家大师讲座等活动全部由学生组织。学校书店、咖啡馆、出版公司等，都由学生自主经营、自负盈亏。学校为学生搭建舞台，舞台的主角永远都是学生。"校园机会榜"是激励学生产生想法的平台，给学生创造更多成功的机会，让学生在不同的活动中找到自我，提高自己的适应能力，激发自己的潜能。

The school expands the space for students to grow independently as much as possible. The Campus Opportunity List is designed to assign proper tasks of organizing student activities through open bidding. Activities such as foreign cultural day, graduation ceremony, adult ceremony, flag raising ceremony, and masters' lectures are all organized by students, and school bookstores, cafes, publishing companies, etc., are also run by students. The school builds one stage after another for students, and the leading characters on stage are always students. The Campus Opportunity List provides a platform that inspires students to generate ideas, and creates more opportunities for students to succeed. Students can find themselves in different activities, improve their adaptability, and stimulate their potential.

戏剧课上负责灯光的同学（2013.01.23）

The student in charge of lighting in the drama class

学校红窗汇期间练摊的同学们（2019.06.14）

Students set up stalls during the Red Window Fair

一年一度的校园歌手大赛（2020.09.30）

The annual campus singer competition

03

平等的学校

A School Built on Equality

◆ 教育本来挺简单，只是我们人为地把它搞复杂了。让校园里充满民主、平等的氛围，让老师、学生在校园里自由呼吸。把孩子们当作活生生的人来看待，视学校如家庭，视教育如生命。

◆ 每一位教师、每一个成人，都应该蹲下身来和孩子说话。

◆ 当我们希望校园里产生更多学生的想法时，一个生机勃勃的校园氛围马上就会诞生，而创新精神自然也会在校园里蓬勃生长。

◆ 师生关系的主导方在教师，教师应该主动承担起建立良好师生关系的责任。

◆ 教育是塑造心灵的艺术。教育的伟大、神圣在此，教育的艰难也在此。

◆ 不要忘记标注姓名。那种被尊重的感觉常常在一个简单的标注中产生，这样的机会管理者一定不要错过。

◆ 在校内的合影，除非外事工作需要，校长尽量不要处在中间位置，因为那样势必使处于边角位置的人感到被忽略。如果校长敢于、乐于把自己放在一个边角、后排的位置，就会使整个照片的位置全都成了好于校长的位置。

- Education is very simple, but we artificially complicate it. Let the campus be filled with a democratic and equal atmosphere, and let teachers and students breathe freely on campus. Treat children as unique individuals, view the school as a family, and education as life.
- Every teacher and adult, should bend down when talking with children.
- When we hope more ideas from students can grow on campus, a vibrant campus atmosphere will be formed immediately, and the spirit of innovation will naturally flourish on campus.
- The teacher-student relationship is dominated by teachers, so teachers should take the initiative and responsibility to establish a good teacher-student relationship.
- Education is the art of shaping mind. This is why education is a great, holy, but also difficult undertaking.
- Don't forget to mark students'names. The feeling of being respected often arises from a simple annotation. Teachers must not miss such an opportunity.
- When taking group photos, unless required by foreign affairs, the principal had better not be in the middle position, because that will inevitably make those in the corners feel ignored. If the principal dares and hopes to position himself in a corner or in the back row, all positions in the photo will be better than the principal's.

平等的师生关系

Equal Teacher-student Relationship

　　平等的师生关系是一切真实教育的基础，十一学校拆掉了所有教室里的讲台，促使老师以平等的姿态面对学生。老师们设立自己的学科教室，将办公桌搬进教室，走入学生中间进行交流，确立师生之间的平等地位。尤其是在实行选课走班、取消班主任后，老师真正成为学生的良师益友，担负着教书育人的职责。在十一学校，学生在老师面前亦可以呈现出真实的自我。

　　Equal teacher-student relationship is the foundation of all real education. BNDS dismantled podiums in all classrooms to encourage teachers to face students on an equal footing. Teachers set up their own subject classrooms, move desks into the classrooms, and approach to communicate with students. An equal status is therefore established between teachers and students. Especially after the implementation of course selection system and the cancellation of head teachers, teachers truly become students' friends with the responsibility of teaching and educating. At BNDS, students can present their true selves in front of teachers.

生物实验室内的泡菜让学生感受到不一样的味道（2012.05.25）

Pickles made in biology lab gives students a different taste

中考送考（2018.06.24）

Sending students to the high school entrance exam

高三毕业谢师会（2021.06.22）

Grade 12 Teacher Appreciation Ceremony

亦师亦友的导师制

The Advisor System Changing Teachers to Friends

十一学校取消行政班后，班主任没有了，取而代之的是导师制。没有了警察式的班主任，学生轻松了许多，也变得更加活泼真实。学校没有了班主任，却提倡"人人都是班主任"——每个老师都应担负起教育的责任，但又不能延续传统的班主任的管理方式。于是，老师们多了一个绝大多数中学老师没有的身份——导师，负责对学生进行人生与职业引导、心理疏导和学业指导。学生经常与导师亲近地会面交谈突破了传统师生关系。亦师亦友，不只是说说而已。

After BNDS canceled the administrative class, head teachers were replaced by advisors. Without the police-style discipline, students are much more relaxed, lively and real. BNDS advocates that "every teacher is a head teacher" instead of head teacher, which means every teacher should take the responsibility for education, but different from what head teachers did in the past. As a result, teachers got an identity that most high school teachers do not have—advisors, who are responsible for students' life and career guidance, psychological counseling and academic guidance. It is a breakthrough of the traditional teacher-student relationship that students have opportunity to meet and communicate closely with their mentors frequently. As a result, teachers become students' real friends.

导师给准备参加高三毕业典礼的同学化妆（2021.06.23）

An advisor did makeup for students preparing for Graduation Ceremony

学 校 的 样 子
WHAT THE SCHOOL LOOKS LIKE

开启中学时光（2015.08.20）

Mark the start of high school life

教师节，同学们为老师们颁发表彰证书。（2021.09.10）

Students awarded recognition certificates to teachers on Teacher's Day

学生内阁的民主意识

Democratic Awareness of the Student Cabinet

　　这是由一群充满热情的学生所组建的学生自治组织，主要工作包括发起各种针对校园生活中存在问题的调查，并将调查结果汇总为改进方案呈报给学校；监督各个学校机构以及学生组织的工作等。另外，学生会定期参加学校的校长办公会，从而使学生的想法得到尊重、理解和实行，这就为学生参与未来的民主生活和民主社会建设奠定了基础。

　　This is a student managed organization formed by a group of enthusiastic students. Its main mission includes launching investigations on problems in campus life, and summarizing the investigation results into improvement plans before submitting to the school. It also supervises the operation of school institutions and student organizations. In addition, students regularly participate in the principal's office meeting, so that their ideas can be respected, understood and implemented, which lays the foundation for students to participate in the future democratic life and democratic society construction.

就学习生活方面的热点问题进行的大讨论（2013.06.04）

General discussion on hot issues in campus life

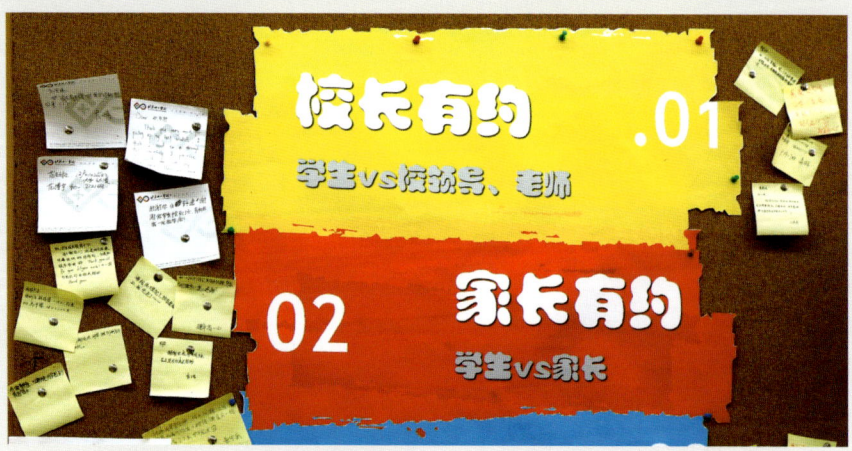

共进午餐的"校长有约"
Lunch with the Principal

　　学校每周一如约进行"校长有约"这项活动，学生通过网上报名来获得与校长共进午餐、面对面进行交流的机会。精致的饭食、多样的选择，让人垂涎欲滴，食欲大开；校长和蔼的笑容，同伴们的谈笑自若，营造了温馨轻松的氛围。午餐中，校长可以及时倾听来自学生的声音。这种民主平等、轻松活泼的沟通氛围，既有利于同学们发出自己的声音，又有助于校长准确把握学生的脉搏，了解学生的真实需求。学生们有想法，有主见，观点丰富新颖，他们不仅反映问题，还积极为学校的发展建言献策。

　　Students can have lunch with the principal every Monday. They can register online to get the opportunity to communicate face-to-face with the principal during lunch. The exquisite and mouth-watering dishes, the principal's kind smile and students' chatting and laughter form a warm and relaxing atmosphere. While eating and chatting, the principal can hear voices of students in time. This democratic, equal and lively communication not only encourages students to express their own voice, but also helps the principal to accurately understand the real needs of students. Students with creative ideas and opinions not only reflect problems of the school, but also actively offer suggestions for better development of the school.

积极建言献策的同学们（2022.03.21）

Students giving advice on a better school life

没有讲台的教室
Classrooms Without Podiums

随着自主选课、走班制度的实施，学生可根据自身实际需求选择课程。课后，学生也可自主选择学科教室进行自习。在这种学生不断流动的情况下，任课教师在管理和教育方面的责任大大增加。每一位教师都从专心于学科教学转变为投入学科教育，他们不仅要负责教授本学科，还要关注学生的心理、情绪和人际交往状况。在学科教学之外承担起教育、管理学生的工作，对于教师而言，是一个契机——走下讲台，走近学生，侧耳倾听他们的内心。

With the implementation of the new course selection system, students can choose courses according to their personal situation. Outside of class time, students can also choose subject classrooms for self-study. With this constant flow of students, the responsibilities of classroom teachers are greatly increased in terms of managing and educating students. Every teacher has changed from focusing exclusively on subject teaching to subject education, meaning that they are not only responsible for teaching the subject, but also for paying attention to students' psychological, emotional and interpersonal conditions. Taking on the work of educating students apart from subject teaching is an opportunity for teachers to step down from the podium, approach students, and listen to their hearts.

选择适合自己层次的课程进行学习（2016.06.04）

Choose courses that suit students themselves

精细化的分布式领导
Refined Distributed Leadership

    为了使学校管理从粗放式向精细化、专业化发展，学校让每位老师都承担起管理者的责任。在年级层面，通过"分布式领导"模式，把教育教学管理事务分解为导师、咨询师、学科教研组长、小学段与研究性学习主管、过程性评价主管、终结评价与诊断主管、选课与排课主管、教育顾问、自主研修主管、考勤主管、大型活动主管等多个岗位。由任课教师根据自己的专长主动承担，既确保了年级工作和教育教学管理的高效、有序，又给每一位教师搭建了施展个人才华的平台。

In order to transform the extensive school management to be more refined and professional, BNDS distributes management responsibilities to every teacher. In each grade, through the "distributed leadership" model, education management work is divided and assigned to different positions such as advisor, consultant, subject teaching director, project and research based learning director, process evaluation director, final evaluation and diagnosis director, course selection and scheduling director, education consultant, self-study director, attendance director, campus event director, and so on. Teachers take the initiative to undertake different positions according to their own expertise, which not only ensures the efficiency and order of education work in each grade, but also builds a platform for teachers to display their personal talents.

隆重表彰上学年贡献突出的老师们（2020.11.28）

Ceremonious recognition of teachers
who made outstanding contributions in the last school year

传承红色基因

Inherit the Gene of "Chinese Red"

北京十一学校于1952年建校，前身是中央军委子弟学校，是唯一一所由周恩来总理批准、中央军委拨款建造、用共和国生日命名的学校，学校开设了"红十一"校史课程，传承建校时的红色精神，让"共和国学校"的红色基因不断传承下去！

Established in 1952, BNDS was the only school named after the National Day of the People's Republic of China. The school has set up school history courses to inherit the patriotic spirit formed when the school was first founded and let the gene of "Chinese red" continue to be passed on.

手持党旗和团旗在学校将帅题词的碑林墙前合影（2021.05.18）

Holding flags in front of the inscriptive monument wall

参加天安门建党百年庆祝活动的同学们整装待发（2021.07.01）

Students participating in national celebration at the Tian'anmen Square

04

自由呼吸的学校
A School Promoting Independence

- 每一个人只有在自由的状态下，才能逐渐学会自律，也只有如此，才能使之学会自主生活。生活在集体之外的时候，每一个个体都需要自我认知，需要明确自己的人生方向和行走方式。

- 校园里一旦放手，教育机会随处可见，而管理的缰绳一旦勒紧，教育便无从下手。如果我们天天盯着孩子，不让他们发生问题，其实，问题并没有真正解决，只是我们让孩子带着这些看不见的东西走上了社会，把这些祸根留给了未来罢了。

- 学生是学习的主人，是我们组织教学的基础。

- 课堂小天地，天地大舞台，我们只有给孩子们营造一个更加广大、多元的学习舞台，他们的未来才值得期待。

- 课堂是分享思想的课堂，分享智慧的课堂。每个人都在积极参与，既帮助了别人，同时也从别人那里获得了启迪。在这一过程中，大家收获的不仅仅是方法，更有思考问题的习惯和方式。

- 什么时候孩子们在我们的课堂上学会独立思考了，什么时候孩子们能够探寻属于自己的答案了，我们的教育也就成功了。

- 当我们把学生最终推向社会的时候，当再也没有人给他讲课的时候，他如何学习，如何工作，如何生活？终身学习的习惯和终身学习的能力，是未来成功人士应具备的最为关键的要素之一。

- Only in a state of freedom can people gradually learn to discipline themselves, and only in this way can they learn to live independently. When living outside the collective, each individual needs self-awareness and needs to clarify his or her own life direction and the way of living.

- Once teachers let go of students, the opportunities of education comes everywhere on campus; once the reins of management are tightened, education will be tough to achieve. If we stare at children every day, preventing them from making mistakes, we are not solving any problem, instead, we are sending students to the society with the invisible problems, leaving potential hazards to the future.

- Students are the masters of learning and the foundation of the education.

- The classroom is a small space but a large platform. Only when we create a broader and more diverse learning platform for children, can their future be worth looking forward to.

- A classroom is a place where ideas and wisdom are shared. Everyone is actively participating, helping and inspiring. In this process, everyone gains not only learning methods, but also habits and ways of thinking.

- Our education is successful only when children in classrooms learn to think independently and explore answers of their own.

- When we finally send students into society, where no one will teach them anymore, how will they learn, work, and live? The habit and ability of lifelong learning are one of the most crucial quality for successful people in the future.

每人一张课程表
Unique Timetable for Every One

　　十一学校在国家课程标准的基础上，开发了一些校本课程，不断地给课程增加宽度、厚度和深度。按照学生将来的不同发展方向，数学、物理、化学、生物等理科课程分三级设置，历史、地理、政治分两级设置，使得学生在适合自己的课程中充分汲取知识。随着课程改革的深入进行，数学课程进一步划分成了数学 I 到数学 V 五个层次，还向上延伸出微积分、线性代数等大学先修课程，向下延伸出援助课程，让所有学生都能找到与自己的能力和需求相适应的课程。

On the basis of the national curriculum standards, BNDS has developed school-based courses, continuously adding width, thickness and depth to the curriculum. According to the different development directions of students in the future, science courses such as mathematics, physics, chemistry, and biology are divided into three levels, and history and geography are divided into two levels, so that students can fully absorb knowledge in the courses suitable for them. With the deepening of the curriculum reform, the mathematics curriculum has been further divided into five levels: Mathematics I to V, plus advanced pre-university courses such as calculus and linear algebra, and supporting courses for students falling behind. All students can find courses suitable for their abilities.

独轮车体育课（2021.07.02）

Unicycle PE class

有针对性的个别化交流

Targeted and Individualized Communication

在十一学校，每座教学楼里都会有许多休闲区，这里是老师和学生进行个别交流的地方。通过个别交流，老师指引学生进行人生规划，理清职业目标和学习目标，启动学生内在动力；通过分类型、分层次的选择性指导，十一学校实现了因材施教和个别化教育，构建了使每一位学生为自己负责的教育机制。

At BNDS there will be many recreational areas in each teaching building, where teachers and students can communicate individually. Through individual communication, teachers guide students to make life plans, clarify career goals and learning goals, and activate students' intrinsic motivation. Through guidance of different types and levels, BNDS educates students in accordance with their aptitude and realizes individualized education. An education system enabling students to be responsible for themselves has therefore been established.

每个年级都设有咨询师，为同学们解答学习、生活中的疑惑。(2012.11.13)

Each grade has a counselor to answer students' doubts in study and life.

学生是课堂的主角
Students Playing the Main Role in Class

　　一直以来，学校坚持课堂教学改革的价值观，在《学校行动纲要》里明确提出了调整教学关系的要求，其中包括：课堂是学生学习的地方，是学生的舞台，并非老师展示自我的地方；减少讲和听，增加说与做。学生已经会的不讲，学生自己能够学会的不讲，讲了学生也不会的不讲。十一学校的课堂形式灵活多样，注重小组讨论、合作探究等环节，对学生实行因材施教，照顾到每一个学生。这样的课堂教学提高了学生小组合作探究、自主解决问题的能力，学生是课堂的主角。

　　All the while, BNDS adheres to the value of classroom teaching reform, and clearly emphasizes the need to adjust teaching and learning relationship in the School Program of Action: the classroom is the place where students learn, and it is the stage for students instead of the showcase for teachers; teachers should reduce the proportion of lecturing in class and increase time for students to practice and discuss; teachers should not teach what students have already known, what they can learn by themselves, or what they can hardly understand. Classes at BNDS are flexible and diverse, focusing on activities like group discussion and cooperative exploration. Teachers care for each individual and teach them in accordance with their different aptitudes. Such classroom teaching methods improve students' ability to explore and solve problems independently in groups. In this way, students play the main role in class.

课堂上在进行小组合作学习的同学们（2018.12.05）

Students in the classroom working on cooperative group learning

现代技术支持的数字化校园
A Digital Campus Supported by Modern Technology

　　数字化校园是实现教育信息化建设的重要途径，十一学校在数字化校园的建设与应用过程中，不单是进行技术上的变革，更重要的是通过信息化教育帮助实现教育思想、教育观念、教育方法的转变，更好地促进学生的个性化发展。数字化校园的建设为选课走班提供了资源准备和技术平台支持，对学生的过程性评价和联络也是借助于多功能的网络技术平台的支撑。此外，全校无线网络覆盖，也为师生的校园生活提供了很大的方便。

Digital campus is an important way to realize the construction of education informatization. In the process of construction and application of digital campus, BNDS not only reformed the technology, but also realized the transformation of educational ideas, concepts and methods through information-based education, thus better promoting students' individualized development. The construction of digital campus provides resource preparation and technical support for the course selection system and students' process evaluation. In addition, the wireless network coverage of the whole campus also provides great convenience for the campus life of teachers and students.

数字技术与教育教学的融合（2017.09.05）

The integration of digital technology and education

名家大师进校园
Famous Masters Visiting the Campus

　　为了启迪学生的成长，每周三下午学校都会举行名家大师进校园活动，这是帮助学生实现"志存高远"这一培养目标的重要课程。有许多位政治、经济、科学、文学、艺术、媒体等方面的名家来学校与学生面对面进行交流互动，讲述自己的成长经历和人生感悟。学生从名家大师的演讲中汲取人生的精华。"一句话能够影响学生的一生。"这样的话多了，教育的力量就大了，学生对于自己的发展方向也就更有主见了。

　　In order to inspire students in their growth, BNDS will invite famous masters to visit every Wednesday afternoon, which is an important course encouraging students to have high aspirations. Famous experts from fields such as politics, economics, science, literature, art, and media come to communicate face-to-face with students, and tell about their growth experiences and life insights. Students draw the essence of life from the famous masters' speeches. "A sentence may affect a student's life". With more sentences like this, education can be more powerful, and students will be more independent and confident when choosing their life directions.

体育名家进校园活动（2020.10.21）

Sports masters participate in campus interaction

学术型的少年科学院
Junior Academy of Sciences

　　学会知识只是学习的一部分，学习更需要的是在原有知识的基础上实践创新，十一学校因此成立了少年科学院，为同学们科学探索搭建起了平台。少年科学院是一个以科学探索为共同志趣的学生社团组织，院长一职由学生担任。与普通社团组织不同的是，学校为少年科学院的小院士们提供进入国家重点实验室进行实践研究的机会。此外，十一学校还成立了少年文学院、少年社科院、少年经济学院等学生自主管理的学院，使更多的学生有机会在自己感兴趣的领域进行学术实践。

　　Gaining knowledge is only one part of learning, and what is more important is to practice and innovate on the basis of the original knowledge. The school therefore established the Junior Academy of Sciences as a platform for students' scientific exploration. Junior Academy of Sciences is a student association led by students with a common interest in scientific exploration. Different from other school clubs, the school provides the young academicians with opportunities to enter National Key Laboratories for practical research. In addition, BNDS has also established other academies independently managed by students, such as Junior Academy of Literature, Junior Academy of Social Sciences, and Junior Academy of Economics, so that more students can have the opportunity to conduct academic practice in their areas of interest.

技术节让学生感受到成功的乐趣（2012.11.13）

Technology Festival gives students a sence of success

可进行深入研究的高端实验室
High-end Labs for Deep Research

  为了给对理科实验有较高要求的学生提供深入研究的机会，学校建立了物理、化学和生物高端实验室，配备了先进的实验仪器，并由相关学科的博士老师进行指导。有些在大学实验室才可以做的实验，学生在这里就可以完成，这些高端实验室为学生创造了更好的学习条件。

In order to provide students who have higher requirements for science experiments with opportunities for in-depth research, the school has established high-end laboratories for physics, chemistry and biology. The laboratories are equipped with advanced experimental instruments and are guided by doctoral teachers in related disciplines. Some experiments that can only be done in university laboratories can be completed by students here. These high-end laboratories have created better learning conditions for students.

学生在化学高端实验室进行研究活动（2014.04.24）

Students conducting research in a high-end chemistry lab

针对个体的枣林村书院

Zaolincun Academy Targeted to Individuals

　　学校成立枣林村书院，主要是为学生创造课程，满足高度个性化的需求。这里的课程都是针对少数学生，甚至是学生自己开设的非常规课程，让一些偏才怪才在这里有用武之地。枣林村书院的成立有助于发现每一位学生的不同，唤醒每一位学生的潜能，启动每一位学生的内动力，让每一位学生成为自我发展的承担者。只有解放了学生，让他们拥有相信自己的力量，他们才能去实现心中的梦想。

　　The school established Zaolincun Academy with the main task of creating courses for students with highly individualized needs. The courses here are all aimed at a small number of students, and there are even unconventional courses open for one student alone. As a place where students with eccentric talents can shine, Zaolincun Academy helps discover things that make each student special, awaken their potential, activate their inner motivation, and make them responsible for self-development. Only by liberating students and giving them the power to believe in themselves can they realize their dreams.

枣林村书院教室内两位同学在交流学习（2021.11.03）

Two students learning and discussing in the classroom of Zaolincun Academy

可自主安排的小学段
Short Period for Personalized Learning

　　为了给学生更多自主选择的空间，学校实施了"大小学段制"。每个学期分两个大学段和一个小学段，大学段主要进行统一课程的集中学习，两个大学段之间的小学段，为期两周，学生仍然到校学习，但不安排统一的学习内容，每位学生根据自己的学习需求，制定出符合自己的自主学习规划，进行自主学习；也有很多学生利用这段时间，走出学校，到社会和实验基地进行实地体验学习。小学段给了每一位学生进行校外社会体验和个性化学习的机会，也使他们的自主学习能力得到锻炼和提升，同样帮助他们学会安排自己的生活。

　　In order to give students more free choices, the school has divided each semester into two long periods and a short period in between. Students have normal classes during the long periods, but have no class during the two-week short period at school. It's a time for them to make personal learning plan according to their own needs; some students also take this chance to go to the society or experimental bases for some practical experiences. The special self-study period enables every student to have personalize learning experiences and social experiences, and it also improves their independent learning ability and self-management ability.

小学段期间在化学教室学习的同学（2016.11.10）

Students studying in the chemistry classroom during the short period

年级组织的拔河比赛（2018.10.04）

Tug of war organized by the grade

满足更高层次学习需求的自主研修学院

Independent Learning Academy for Higher Level Learning Needs

　　十一学校设有自主研修学院，提供上不封顶的课程支持以满足学生更高层次的学习需求。学院对自主发展意识、学习能力、自我管理能力等方面均较强的学生开放，配备各学科导师及人生规划指导教师。经过教师同意，学生们可以随时使用学院各种教室、图书资料、电脑、网络等资源。另外，以独立研修为主，小组讨论为辅，同一研修课题的学员可以在导师指导下组成自主合作研修小组集体讨论有关问题，或者与导师商讨学习计划、研究学习中的难题，等等。

BNDS has an Independent Learning Academy to meet unlimited learning needs of students. The academy is open, which opens to students with strong self-development awareness, learning ability, and self-management ability, and is equipped with academic tutors and life planning instructors. With the consent of teachers, students can use various classrooms, library materials, computers, networks and other resources at the academy at any time. Independent study is the main learning method here, supplemented by group discussions. Students with the same study topic can form an independent cooperative study group under the guidance of their instructors to discuss relevant issues, and they can also discuss with their instructors about study plans and research problems in the study.

学校为同学们自主研修创造了一些不同特色的空间 (2017.03.10)

The school has created spaces with various designs for students' independent study

努力实现由教走向学

Striving to Realize the Transition from Teacher-oriented to Student-oriented Class

　　十一学校一直着眼于课堂变革，力求通过基于课标、重构单元、确立目标、设计任务、改进评估，探索如何在课堂上落实学科核心素养，实现从教学到学习的深度转型。课堂上教师给学生自主体验探究的机会，老师给学生提供工具、学习任务、学习目标等资源，调动学生的内动力，引导学生在自主学习和深度体验中，学会解决问题的方法策略，提高课堂效率。

　　BNDS has been focusing on classroom reform, and strives to explore how to implement the core competences of disciplines in class by following curriculum standards, restructuring units, setting goals, designing tasks, and optimizing assessments, so as to achieve an in-depth transformation from teaching to learning. In the classroom, teachers give students the opportunity to experience and explore independently. They provide students with resources including tools, learning tasks, and learning objectives to mobilize students' internal motivation. They guide students to learn problem-solving methods and strategies through independent learning and in-depth experience, thus improving efficiency in class teaching.

化学课堂上积极提问的同学（2014.03.14）

Students actively asking questions in chemistry class

为了帮助同学们自主学习，老师们进行学习单元开发。（2018.03.14）

Teachers conduct learning unit research and
development to facilitate independent learning

05

寻找同伴的学校
A School for
Life-long Friendship

◆ 最容易成为终生朋友的，往往是在人生观、价值观和世界观形成的关键时期，也就是中学时期结识的同伴。

◆ 社会化是具体的，找到同伴并成为日后踏入社会的同盟或志同道合的朋友，正是教育的本义之一。

◆ 要重视学生情感的培养，特别是重视学生积极人生态度的培养，重视团队精神、合作意识、良好同伴关系的培养，让学生学会妥协。

◆ 当我们的孩子在内心深处明确地认定自己不属于任何人，可以在许多团队中扮演不同的角色时，他们才真正长大，也逐步有了一些公民的样子，这时候，他们的肩上也就有了沉甸甸的责任。

◆ 在学校的实际工作中，我们特别注意构建"我们"的团队，大量的工作都是以项目团队的方式推进，从课程开发到教学组织方式设计，从管理结构的重建到评价制度的形成，团队的智慧让每一个成员都感受到了"我们"的力量。

◆ 教育正是为了避免单独平面的思维而存在，不同生活经验的孩子们聚集在校园里，各不相同的观点互相碰撞。越是多元，越是让学生见怪不怪；越是多元，越有利于学生从偏激走向成熟；越是多元，越有利于各种个性的人才自由地成长。

- Companions in high school are the most likely to become lifelong friends, as high school is a critical period for people to form an outlook on world and life values.

- Socialization is concrete, and finding companions and becoming like-minded allies who step into society together in the future is one of the original intention of education.

- It is necessary to attach importance to the cultivation of students' emotions, especially positive attitudes towards life, such as team spirit, sense of cooperation, good peer relationships, spirit of tolerance and compromise.

- Our children will truly grow up and be able to take on the responsibility of citizenship when they feel in their hearts that they don't belong to anyone and can play different roles in many teams.

- At BNDS, we pay special attention to constructing "our" team. A lot of work is carried out by different project teams. From curriculum development and teaching planning, to reconstructing management structure and forming evaluation system, the collective wisdom of teams makes every member feel "our" power.

- Education exists precisely for avoiding thinking from a single angle. Children with different life experiences gather on campus with different viewpoints colliding and integrating with one another. The more diverse the viewpoints, the easier it is for students to accept, and the more helpful it is for students to move from being extreme to being mature and to grow freely with various talents and personalities.

丰富多彩的社团活动
Colorful Club Activities

　　社团是学校综合实践课程中的一门自选课程，学生创办社团、参加社团活动可以获得综合实践课程学分。社长主持一个社团，每个学期最多可以获得1.3学分；社员参与社团活动，每个学期最多可以获得0.8学分。十一学校社团在200个左右，包括体育运动、艺术表演、慈善公益、自然科学、社会科学等十五大类，各有特色。社团活动不仅让志同道合的同学组建团队，获得归属感，还能让同学们亲身体验一个组织的建立和管理，为同学们提供宝贵的实践平台和展示机会。

Club is an optional course in school's comprehensive practice courses. Students can obtain course credits by starting a club or participating in club activities. The president of a club can earn up to 1.3 credits per semester, and members who participate in club activities can earn up to 0.8 credits per semester. The number of BNDS clubs has been stabilized at about 200, which can be divided into 15 general categories such as sports, art performances, charity, natural sciences, and social sciences. Each club with its distinctive characteristics complements each other. Club activities not only allow like-minded students to find a team and gain a sense of belonging, but also allow students to experience the establishment and management of an organization, providing students with valuable practice platforms and opportunities to show themselves.

橡皮章社团招新（2019.06.14）

Rubber Stamp Design Club recruiting members

学生乐队招新（2019.09.12）

Student Band recruiting members

微电影社团推介学校开设的影视编导课程（2014.03.12）

Microfilm Club introducing the film and television choreography course

涉及不同领域的职业考察课程
Career Inspection Courses Covering Different Fields

十一学校帮助学生从个性、志趣、特长，到多元智能、情商等方面了解自己，还帮助他们认识社会，特别是让他们进行系统的职业考察。学校把从业人员最多的近 30 个行业作为重点，开发学生职业考察课程，涵盖金融、经济、信息技术、文化出版等多个不同领域。每一种职业由一位老师担任考察顾问，在每一个学年里安排 4 次考察活动，让学生根据自己的需要选择参与。职业考察课程是帮助学生走出校园，通向社会的一条通径。

BNDS helps students to understand themselves in terms of personality, interests, specialties, multiple intelligences, emotional intelligence, etc. The school also helps them understand the society, and especially allows them to conduct systematic career investigations. The school focuses on nearly 30 industries with the largest number of employees, and has developed student career inspection courses, covering many different fields such as finance, economics, information technology, and cultural publishing. For each occupation, a teacher serves as an inspection consultant, and four inspection activities are held in each academic year, allowing students to participate according to their own needs. Career inspection courses provide a broad path to help students step out of the campus and find their position in the society.

去超市进行职业体验（2012.05.20）

Visiting a supermarket for vocational experience

创设可供交流的公共空间
Public Spaces for Communication

　　在十一学校的校园里，精心设计了许多富有特色的公共空间，课余时间学生们会选择自己喜欢的空间，和伙伴一起讨论问题、制定计划、交换信息，学校俨然成为学生的公共社区。在充满选择的校园和课程中，学生可以找到更多的同伴，尤其是有着共同爱好的同伴。在自由宽松的环境里，学生渐渐学会了"对自己负责、对同伴负责，对周围环境乃至社会负责"。

　　On the campus of BNDS, many distinctive public spaces are carefully designed. During spare time, students will choose their favorite spaces to discuss, make plans, and exchange information with like-minded partners. The school has become a public community for students. On a campus full of choices, students can find more companions, especially those who share common interests. In a free and relaxed environment, students gradually learn to be "responsible for themselves, for their peers, for the surrounding environment, and even the society."

校友在母校缘宫举办婚礼（2018.05.01）

Alumni holding their wedding at the Hall of Ties

同学们在小空间学习交流（2021.03.08）

Students studying and communicating in a small space

发挥学术力量的教育家书院
Educator Academy that Unleashes Academic Power

学校成立了教育家书院，运用学术的力量进行教师专业培训，有针对性地破解改革中遇到的难题，提高教师的业务水平。教育家书院不提倡几百人的集训，一般为选择性课程，让老师去选择。这貌似低效，却是可持续的、有针对性的。十一学校有大批优秀教师，以教育家的情怀、教育家的境界、教育家的心态和教育家的教育艺术来推动学校发展、影响学生成长。

The school has established the Educator Academy, where academic powers are gathered to conduct professional training for teachers, solve problems encountered in the reform, and improve the teaching ability of teachers. The Educator Academy does not advocate training for hundreds of people, but offers selective courses for teachers to choose. Such teacher training courses seem inefficient, but they are sustainable and of strong pertinence. BNDS has a large number of outstanding teachers who promote the development of the school and influence students' growth with the attitude, mentality, and art of qualified educators.

盟校间的圆桌论坛活动（2016.08.25）

Roundtable forum activities among allied schools

狂欢节上老师们的特色装扮（2017.12.29）

The special costumes of teachers at the carnival

教育年会圆桌论坛（2017.08.26）

Round table at the Education Forum

和谐的同伴关系日
Harmonious Companionship Day

　　在充满选择的校园里，学生们可以找到更多的同伴，尤其是有共同爱好的同伴。每一位学生每个学期都会选择在近十个不同的群体里学习、生活，这扩大了学生的交往范围，也促使学生在每一个团队重新寻找自己的位置，扮演不同的角色，承担自己的责任。在这种环境中，和谐的同伴关系对学生的成长发展至关重要。为了促进学生关系的正确发展，学校设立了"同伴关系日"，以发展良好的同伴关系，营造友好的校园氛围。

　　On a campus full of choices, students can find more companions, especially those who share common interests. With a curriculum full of choices, every student will choose to study and live in nearly ten different groups every semester, which expands the scope of their communication and prompts them to refind their own roles, positions, and responsibilities in each team. In this environment, harmonious peer relationships are essential to the growth and development of students. In order to promote better development of student relationships, the school has set up a "Companionship Day" to develop good peer relationships and create a friendly campus atmosphere.

我们是同学（2021.09.06）

We are classmates

让我仔细看看你（2013.12.23）

Let me take a closer look at you

参加成人礼（2020.12.19）

Attending the Adult Ceremony

W学 校 的 样 子
HAT THE SCHOOL LOOKS LIKE

十一学校盟校篮球比赛（2021.11.27）

BNDS School League Basketball Tournament

06

学生做主的学校

A School Driven by Students

◆ 促使学生自我教育的教育才是真正的教育。

◆ 尊重是开展一切教育活动的前提。

◆ 坚持主体教育，学生能做的，教师不要包办。构建每一位学生为自己的成长负责的教育机制。

◆ 如果我们希望学生真正具有责任感，就应该帮助他找到那些他所关心的事情，他关心的事情越多，他的责任心所及的范围才有可能越大。

◆ 在我们的教育理想里，真正的特色学校应该是让每一位学生都富有个性，都能在校园里找到属于自己独特的成长之路，课程的丰富性、多样性可以支撑各种不同需求的孩子的成长，尽管我们离这样的理想还有很大的距离，但却不能因为眼下难以完全实现而放弃这样的努力，甚至走向一条离这样的目标越来越远的反向的道路。

◆ 尊重学生，尊重他们的想法，尊重他们的个性，尊重他们的处境，倾听他们的声音，和着他们的心跳想事情、做事情，教室里就会变得生机勃勃、春意盎然。

- The real education propels students to educate themselves.
- Respect is a prerequisite for all educational activities.
- We will adhere to students-leading education, in which teachers should not interfere with what students can do by themselves. We will build an educational mechanism where each student is responsible for his or her own growth.
- If we want students to have a real sense of responsibility, we should help them find the things they care about. The more things they care about, the greater the scope of their responsibility.
- In our educational ideals, a school with special characteristic should be a place where every student can flourish with their unique characteristic and find their own growing path. The school should provide diversified curriculum to support students' various needs of growth. Although we still have a long way to achieve this goal, we cannot give up simply because it is hard to achieve at the moment, or even turn to a reverse path farther and farther away from such a goal.
- We should respect students. Respect their ideas, personalities, and situations, listen to their voices, and encourage them to think and take actions following their heartbeat. In this way, the classroom will become full of enthusiasm and vitality.

40 多款校服供学生选择
Over 40 Models of School Uniforms to Choose From

　　和许多中学仍坚持统一的运动款式校服不同，十一学校鼓励学生创建校服文化中心，推出的校服包括休闲类、制式类和运动类，每一类别里有不同的款式，同款式又有不同颜色和不同长短规格，加起来共有 40 余款供学生们选择，深受同学们欢迎，也得到了家长的好评。款式各异的校服有统一的标志，既不违背学校的管理与规范，又尊重了学生的选择权，给学生彰显个性留有余地。靓丽多彩的校服构成了十一校园里一道独特的风景。

　　Unlike most schools that provide the same type of school uniform, BNDS encouraged students to set up a school uniform culture center. They designed different types of uniform such as casual wear, formal wear and sports wear. There are different styles in each category, and different colors, lengths and sizes in each style. Altogether over 40 models are provided for students to choose, which are well received and praised by students and parents. As all uniforms have a unified BNDS logo, wearing different uniforms will not violate the school norms and management, but respects students' right to choose, leaving room for students to show their individuality. The beautiful and colorful school uniforms become a unique scenery on BNDS campus.

学生组织的新版校服发布会（2014.05.25）

Student organizing the launch of new school uniforms

由学生大使来接待校外客人

Student Ambassadors Receiving Guests

　　十一学校的外事活动比较频繁，承担外事活动的不只是学校领导，"接待客人"被精心开发成一门特色课程，"十一学生大使团"应运而生。学生们以自己富有创意的方式，向来自四面八方的参观者展示学校的办学特色，展示自己的风采。即便是接待外国驻华大使，校长也只是在迎接与送别时体现他的存在，致辞、陪同之类的任务都交给了学生。这不仅给了学生锻炼自我、展示自我的机会，更体现了学生才是学校的主人。

External and International communication activities are frequent at BNDS. "Guests hospitality" was designed into a special course, and the "Student Ambassador Association" is therefore established. In their own creative ways, students introduce special characteristics of BNDS to guests from all over the world. Even when receiving foreign ambassadors to China, the principal only present when welcoming and sending off the guests. Students take up tasks such as giving welcoming speeches and leading the campus tour, which not only provides students with the opportunity to show themselves, but also displays that students are the genuine masters of the school.

同学们接待外国客人（2017.11.18）

Students receiving international guests

靠创意赚钱的"校服熊"
Creative School Uniform Bears for Sale

　　在 2012 年的狂欢节期间，十一学校青年成就社团的学生把学校"微缩版"校服穿在小熊玩偶身上，制作成"校服熊"售卖。萌萌的小熊穿上熟悉的校服，格外惹人喜爱，"校服熊"立刻成为最抢手的明星产品。校服熊的出现和经营皆来自学生们的创意实践，销售额达 1.6 万元。最终这笔钱被用于设立"乐群奖学金"，专门奖励处于成长期的小社团。

　　During the 2012 Carnival, students from the Youth Achievement Club wore a "miniature" school uniform on a bear doll, calling it the "school uniform bear". The lovely bears wearing a familiar school uniform immediately became the most sought-after star. The brilliant idea of producing and selling "school uniform bears" comes from students' creative practice, and the club earned 16,000 yuan in this business. The money was finally used to set up the "Lequn Scholarship" to reward the small school clubs that keep developing healthily.

学生设计的校服熊非常畅销（2012.10.04）

The school uniform bear turned to be a hit product

海报成为校园的一道风景

Posters Becoming a Scenery on Campus

　　十一学校的活动很多，包括学术交流、名家讲座、社团活动等，因此学校的各类海报也就比较多，分布在校园的各个角落，这些大大小小的海报一般都是由学生设计的，在立意、色彩、造型等方面都颇有创意，且附有设计者的名字。在这个灵感经常迸发的校园里，设计感十足的海报已成为一道亮丽的风景。

As BNDS holds various activities such as academic exchanges, lectures, and club activities, posters are displayed everywhere on campus. The posters designed by students are quite creative in terms of conception, color, and shape, and the designer's names are attached to them. On this campus where inspiration keeps bursting out, posters with artistic design have become a beautiful scenery.

校园戏剧节海报（2013.07.27）

Posters of Campus Drama Festival

校园主持人大赛海报（2021.11.25）

Poster of Campus Host Contest

美味多多的学生餐厅
Delicious Student Restaurants

　　用餐也是学校内非常重要的事情，学校餐厅面向社会公开招标，引进三家优质餐饮公司来经营，创新经营模式，这样既能保证学生的一日三餐营养，增强学生的体质，又能督促饭菜质量提升，形成良性循环。在不同的学生餐厅以及不同的窗口，学生们可以品尝到不同的风味餐，满足学生的不同口味。

Meals are also important at BNDS. The school restaurants are open to the public for bidding, and three high-quality catering companies have been introduced to manage the restaurants. This innovative business model can not only ensure the nutrition of students' three meals a day and enhance their physical fitness, but also help to supervise the quality of meals, thus forming a virtuous circle. At different restaurants and windows, students can enjoy delicacy with various flavors to satisfy their appetite.

不同的窗口有不同的特色（2021.12.24）

Different windows offer different specialties

积极向上的学生风貌
Positive Student Outlook

　　走进十一学校，你会发现这里的学生轻松活泼、阳光自信，脸上洋溢着笑容。十一学子有热情、有活力、有想法，充分显示出当代中学生蓬勃向上、积极进取的精神风貌。在十一学校，你会感觉到学生是这个学校真正的主人。

　　When walking into BNDS, you will notice that students here are lively, cheerful, and confident with beaming smiles on their faces. BNDS students are enthusiastic, energetic and thoughtful. They demonstrate the vigorous and positive spirit of contemporary high school students. At BNDS, you will feel that the students are the genuine masters of the school.

快乐的中学时光（2017.09.08）

Happy high school life

课外活动时间在操场跑步的师生（2021.09.29）

Students and teachers are jogging after class

成人礼宣誓（2019.12.20）

Vowing to be a responsible adult at the Adult Ceremony

体育季活动（2012.05.29）

Sports Season Activities

07

注重体验的学校

A School Encouraging
Hands-on Experience

◆ 对课程的选择，同样需要我们及早地给学生一些体验。过去那种小学、中学一味必修，而把选择能力的培养全部寄希望于大学的做法，不仅给学生带来能力上的缺失，而且，养成不良的单调的思维方式也是贻害无穷的。

◆ 一个人只有敢于也能够在波诡云谲的人生中扮演不同的角色，他的人生才是安全的，也才有可能是丰富多彩的。

◆ 让学校变得更像一个社会，更像那个未来同学们必须赖以生存的环境，校园里小池塘的水温、水深与将来那个社会大海洋里的水温、水深越是接近、我们的孩子便越是容易生存，也越可能有顺畅的人生。

◆ 我们在管理过程中，在资源分配的过程中，在经费使用的过程中，常常忘了应该集中力量办一些和学生有关的事情，把钱花在离学生最近的地方。

◆ 每一个被管理者都是一个活生生的个体，你不把被管理者放在应有的位置上尊重他们，理解他们，甚至热爱他们，你的管理就不会有太大的成效。管理，其实是组织才华的艺术，又是开发才华的艺术。一个管理者，更应该注意欣赏才华，使才华最大限度地升值，这里面有着管理的很高的境界。

- We should offer students various experience as early as possible through the selection of courses. In the past, primary and secondary schools only offer compulsory courses, leaving the responsibility of fostering students' choice-making ability to university education. Such curriculums not only lead to students' deficiency in ability, but also bring about monotonous thinking habit, leaving endless troubles to future.

- Only when a person dares and is able to play different roles on the turbulent life path, can he or she gain a peaceful and colorful life.

- Let the school become more like the society, an environment where students must inhabit in future. The closer the depth and temperature of the small pond at school are to those of the ocean in society, the easier it will be for children to survive and have a smooth life in the future.

- In the process of school management, resource allocation and funds expenditure, we may forget to concentrate on student-related affairs and spend money on students.

- Everyone being managed is a unique individual. If you don't put them in a proper position, respecting them, understanding them and loving them, your management will not be highly effective. Management is actually the art of organizing and exploiting talents. An outstanding manager should pay more attention to appreciating talents and maximizing the value of talents.

总有角色适合你的戏剧课

Drama Class where Everyone Can Find a Role

　　十一学校开设了种类众多的艺术课，戏剧课便是其中之一。同学们可以根据自己的兴趣特长，在戏剧课中选择表演、舞美、配乐等不同的分工。戏剧课程涉及音乐、美术、影视、舞蹈、文学等相关内容，可供同学们选择的剧目有《花木兰》、《High School Musical》(英文版)、《猫》、《雷雨》、《茶馆》、《三岔口》、《贵妃醉酒》等。同学们在编导、排演不同剧目的过程中提高对艺术的感受力、鉴赏力和创造力，在表达、沟通、团队合作及树立自信心方面得到了发展。

　　BNDS offers a wide variety of art classes, including the drama class. Students can take up different responsibilities in a drama class based on their own interests and strengths, such as performance, choreography, soundtrack, etc. Drama courses involve music, art, film and television, dance, literature and other related contents. The repertoires available for students to choose include *Mulan*, *High School Musical*, *Cat*, *Thunderstorm*, *The Tea House*, *Divergence*, *the Drunken Concubine* and so on. Students improve artistic sensibility, appreciation and creativity in the process of choreographing, directing and rehearsing different plays, and develop confidence and abilities of expression, communication, and teamwork through artistic creation.

戏剧课《花木兰》展演（2013.12.24）

Drama class *Mulan* Showcase

参加戏剧《四世同堂》演出的同学们（2021.07.02）

Students in the performance of *Four Generations under One Roof*

注重体验的学校 A School Encouraging Hands-on Experience   157

学校剧场内的演出（2017.04.20）

Dress-up performance in the school theater

开辟职业体验基地
Career Experience Base

　　学校在教学区开辟了职业体验基地，涉及广告公司、书店、咖啡厅、学生电视台、动漫工作室、汽车设计、服装设计、烹饪等多个领域。寒暑假期间，学生则可以到校外基地，亲身参与职业体验。学校也建议学生在自己选定的领域开展研究性学习和社会实践活动，以便对自己选择的职业有进一步的了解。

　　The school has opened up a career experience base in the teaching area, involving fields of advertising company, bookstore, coffee shop, student TV station, animation studio, car design, clothing design, cooking and so on. During winter and summer vacations, students have chances to participate in career experience at the off-campus base. Students gain different knowledge through the experience, and the school also recommends that students carry out research studies and social practice activities in their chosen fields, so as to have a further understanding of the career prospects.

走过路过不要错过（2012.06.19）

Pass not to miss

获得成就感的红窗汇

Getting a Sense of Achievement from Red Window Fair

　　红窗汇是学校大型活动之一，是课程学习成果的展示、交流、分享和变现的平台，是同学们从学习中获得成就感和认同感的独特方式。红窗汇的名称来源于学校标志性的红色建筑，每一扇红色的窗户里每一天都在发生着生动的学习故事，都在孕育着精彩的学习产品，将这些产品汇集在一起进行交易和分享，就是"红窗汇"啦。

　　The Red Window Fair is one of the biggest school events. It is a platform for displaying, exchanging, sharing and trading students'learning results. It is a unique way of gaining a sense of achievement and recognition from daily study. Red Window Fair is inspired by the iconic red building on campus. At BNDS, wonderful "learning stories" take place every day in every red window. At the Red Window fair, learning products are brought together for trading and sharing.

练摊（2020.09.30）

Street vending

W 学校的样子

熙熙攘攘的红窗汇（2021.06.18）

Bustling Red Window Fair

注重交流的学长有约

Appointment with Seniors

　　学长有约是一项由学生成长服务中心推出的，以与优秀学长谈话的形式，来解决同学们日常学习生活中困惑的活动。参加活动的学长有各年级品学兼优的同学，有学校活动的组织创办者，还有学校各大社团的社长等。与学长谈话的学生则有不知如何适应学校生活的新生，也有在学习上有困惑的高年级学生。学长有约所谈的话题内容广泛，包括日常生活、社团活动、人际关系、理想志向等，为学生与学长自由交流、分享经验提供了平台。

　　Appointment with seniors is an activity launched by the Student Growth Service Center to solve students' confusion in daily learning and life through communication with outstanding seniors. The seniors who participate in the activity include students in all grades with excellent academic performance, founders of school activities, and presidents of clubs. Those who communicate with them range from freshmen who want to adjust to school life to senior students who are confused about their study. The communication covers a wide range of topics, including daily life, social activities, interpersonal relationships, ideals and aspirations, etc., providing a platform for students and seniors to freely communicate and share experiences.

面对面的学长有约活动（2020.11.24）

Face-to-face Appointment with Seniors

毕业年级的入境教育

Preparation Education for Grade 12 Students

　　对于毕业年级的学生，年级会组织开展校外的拓展活动，包括体验式的团队拓展、才艺展示、远程徒步等。通过参与体验、分享总结、反思整合、应用与实施，将乏味、深奥的理论与快乐、刺激的户外体验学习有机地结合起来，对学生们的生存能力、创造能力、展示能力、协作意识、情感修养等进行训练，而且有利于培养学生的吃苦精神和顽强毅力。

For new grade 12 students, the school will organize off-campus development activities, including team building, talent show, hiking, etc. When students participate in the activities, sharing and summarizing, reflecting and practicing, the boring and obscure theories are combined with joyful and stimulating outdoor experiences. These activities enhance students' empathy, creativity, survival ability, presentation ability and collaboration awareness, and is also conducive to cultivating students' spirit of enduring hardship and tenacious perseverance.

拓展活动（2018.07.11）

Development and training activities

我们是一起走过的伙伴（2018.07.13）

We are hand-in-hand partners

体验劳动快乐的开心农场
Feeling the Joy of Labor on the Happy Farm

劳动教育是发挥劳动的育人功能，对学生进行热爱劳动、热爱劳动人民的教育活动。十一学校在校园内操场边的空地开发了"开心农场"学生劳动实践基地，在这里种植了玉米、萝卜、大白菜、黄瓜、胡萝卜等常见的蔬菜瓜果。学生们利用课余时间在这里平整土地、播种育苗、施肥除草、浇水捉虫，锻炼劳动能力，培养吃苦耐劳、艰苦朴素的品格。

Labor education gives full play to the educative function of farm work, and reminds students to appreciate labor and the laborers. BNDS has opened the labor practice base called the "Happy Farm" beside the school stadium, where corns, turnips, cabbages, cucumbers, carrots and other common vegetables and fruits are grown. Students spend their spare time to level the land, sow seedlings, fertilize, weed, and water. The farm exercises students' labor ability and cultivates students' spirit of living a simple and hardworking life.

开垦专属于自己的实验田（2021.03.18）

Exploiting our own experimental field

每个实验田都有不同的名字（2021.07.02）

Each experimental field has a different name

将校友交流设计为课程

Changing Alumni Communication into a Course

　　十一学校倡导处处是课程、时时有课程的大课程观。学校所有的教育教学活动和管理工作都作为课程进行系统设计、深度开发。学校将校庆活动和校友聚会也设计成课程。学校的校庆不是召开大会，而是设计一系列特色活动，注重校友之间的交流。平常也会按照不同的行业组织校友聚会，邀请各行各业的校友和在校学生交流。

　　BNDS advocates a broad course view that lessons can occur anywhere and anytime. All the educational activities and school management work are systematically designed and developed into courses. The school has also developed school anniversary celebrations and alumni gatherings into courses. The school doesn't hold meetings on anniversary day, but set up a series of special activities, focusing on communication between alumni. Alumni gatherings are also organized in normal school days. Outstanding alumni from different fields are invited to communicate with students.

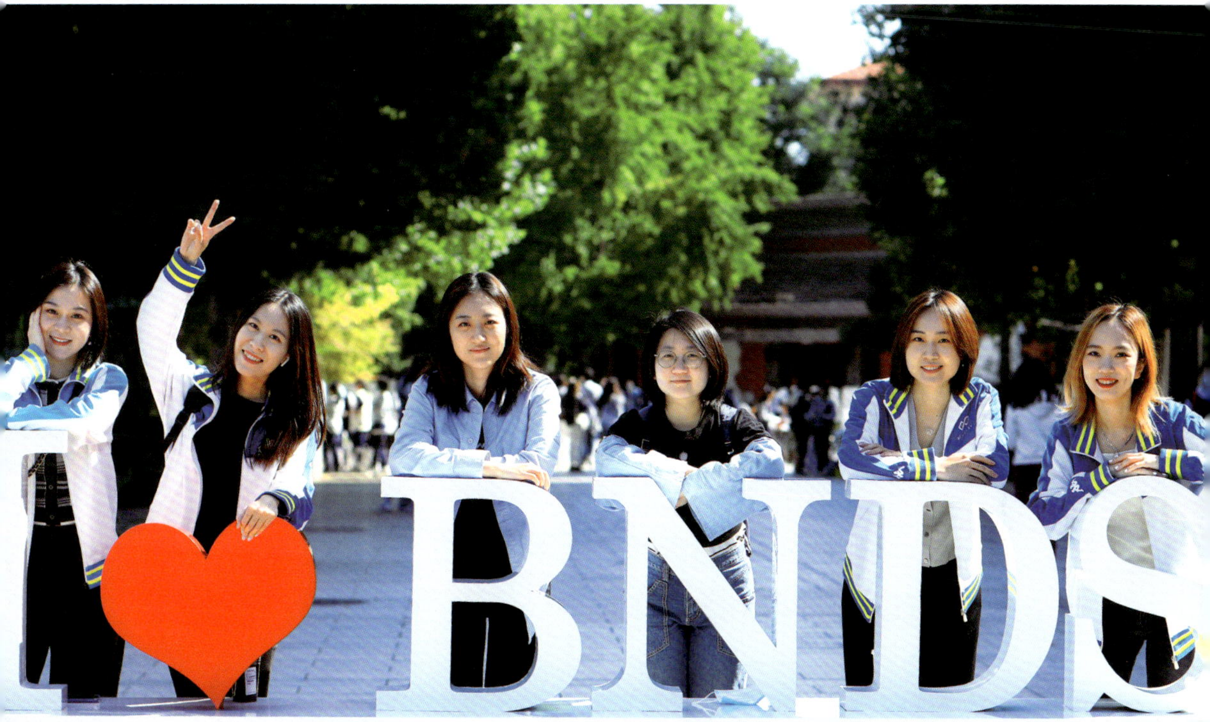

国庆节举办的校友返校活动（2021.10.01）

Alumni homecoming event held on National Day

体验式的拓展活动
Outdoor Development Training for Teachers

　　学校每个学年都会组织新入职的青年教师进行户外拓展，包括多个活动项目，在训练的同时进行总结。学校通过体验式的团队拓展使青年教师加强相互了解，增强团队意识。这不单纯是一种训练，更是一种文化、一种精神、一种理念。青年教师必会将此精神融汇到日后的工作生活中，注重团结协作、进取奉献，为教育事业贡献自己的力量。

Every year the school organizes outdoor development training for newly recruited teachers. The training with various activities enables young teachers to strengthen mutual understanding and enhance team awareness. More than a training, this activity is also a culture, spirit and philosophy, which young teachers should integrate into their future work and life, reminding them to pay attention to cooperation and dedication, and contribute their own strength to education.

参加拓展活动的青年教师（2014.07.10）

Young teachers participating in Outdoor Training

08

国际化的学校

A School for International Vision

◆ 我们不仅在办一所学校，也不只是办好一所学校，我们需要杰出人物凝聚在一起，去完成一项使命：培养更多的能改变这个世界的公民，以及把人类领向美好明天的领军人物。

◆ 引进整合国际优质课程，积极开发与实施国际课程，在可能的领域里努力实现中外课程的融合。

◆ 没有教师积极的情感，就不可能培养出具有健康情感的学生。学校不仅要成为学生向往的地方，更要成为教师向往的地方。

◆ 教师是在学生未来对社会的贡献中寻找自己的人生价值。

◆ 对一个人来说，宽容不同可能已属难能可贵；但对一个民族来说，创造更多的不同，为情趣各异的人们提供不同的生活空间和发展空间可能更加迫切。

◆ 伟大的学校应该是一所师生品格崇高、才识卓越并具有谦虚品质的学校。

◆ 建设国际化学校，培养具有中国灵魂、世界眼光和多元文化理解能力的一流人才。

- We're not just running a school, or striving to build an ideal school, we need luminaries to come together on a mission: to cultivate more citizens who can change the world and lead humanity to a better future.

- We introduce and integrate high-quality international programs, actively develop and implement international curriculum, and strive to achieve the integration of Chinese and international curriculum as far as possible.

- Without teachers' positive emotions, it will be impossible to educate students with healthy emotions. The school must not only be a place students yearn for, but also a place teachers yearn for.

- Teachers find their own value of life in their students' future contribution to society.

- It is by no means easy for a person to tolerate differences, and for a nation, it is even more urgent and valuable to create more differences and provide varied spaces for living and development to people with different characters and interests.

- A great school should be one in which teachers and students have strong moral fiber, outstanding talents, and modest qualities.

- We aim to build an internationalized school and cultivate first-class talents with Chinese soul, world view and multicultural understanding ability.

常态化的国际交流
Normalized International Communication

　　培养具有国际视野、通晓国际规则、能够参与国际事务与国际竞争的国际化人才，是《国家中长期教育改革和发展规划纲要（2010-2020 年)》提出的战略目标。经过多年的探索和实践，十一学校逐渐形成了国际化特色课程。学校有来自不同国家的优秀外籍教师 70 多人，经常开展不同形式的外事活动，进行国际交流。眼光决定人生的高度，十一学校努力将学生培养成具有世界眼光，能担负起国家发展重担的优秀人才。

　　Cultivating international talents who have an international vision, understand international rules, and can participate in international affairs and competition is the strategic goal proposed by the National Medium- and Long-term Education Reform and Development Plan (2010-2020). After years of exploration and practice, BNDS has gradually formed an curriculum with international characteristics. The school has more than 70 outstanding foreign teachers from different countries. Moreover, the school implements various international exchange and communication activities on a regular basis. As vision determines height of life, BNDS strives to cultivate students to become excellent talents with a global vision and capable of shouldering the responsibility of national development.

带你们逛逛我们的校园（2016.10.19）

Show you around our campus

国际交流活动（2017.11.10）

International communication activities

W学校的样子
HAT THE SCHOOL LOOKS LIKE

很高兴认识你（2012.06.20）

Nice to meet you

学生咨询中心
College Counseling Center

　　为帮助有出国留学意向的学生选择适合的大学，国际部成立了学生咨询中心，安排了来自国内外的专职咨询师负责这项工作。学生咨询中心的主要职能是对学生进行理想、心理、学业等方面的咨询指导，根据不同学生的实际情况有针对性地帮助他们选择大学和专业，并帮助他们解决在准备过程中遇到的困难。

　　In order to help students willing to study abroad choose a suitable university, BNDS International Department has established a College Counseling Center (CCC). Full-time Chinese and foreign consultants at CCC provide students with psychological and academic guidance, help them choose universities and majors according to their actual situation, and help them solve difficulties encountered during preparation and college application.

外国高校招生咨询会（2016.09.26）

Admission counseling session for foreign universities

丰富多彩的文化活动
Colorful Cultural Activities

　　国际部逐渐形成具有自己特色的环境文化和管理文化，开展了一系列富有创新性和影响力的文化活动。增强了师生的凝聚力，提高了教育教学的效果。十一学校国际部着力培养具有中国灵魂、世界眼光和多元文化理解力的优秀人才，每年会有许多学生升入世界名牌大学。

BNDS International Department has gradually created its unique environmental and management culture. The International Department strives to cultivate outstanding talents with Chinese soul, global view and multi-cultural understanding ability. Many students are admitted to world top universities every year.

参加演出的同学们（2018.04.19）

Students in the show

合唱演出（2015.05.28）

Choir performance

体育季（2018.10.12）

Sports season

高三毕业留念（2015.06.13）

Teachers and graduates

中外结合的师资力量

Joint Efforts by Chinese and Foreign Teachers

　　国际部拥有一支高素质、高水平、可持续发展的中外教师团队。中外教师拥有丰富的教育教学经验，致力于国际教育，都毕业于中外著名高校。他们博学风趣，精心设计每一堂课，关注每个学生的成长，为学生获取终身的学习力奠定基础。

The International Department has a high-quality, professional and sustainable team of Chinese and foreign teachers. Graduated from top Chinese and foreign universities, teachers at the International Department have rich experience in education, and are committed to develop better international education. The humorous and erudite teachers carefully arrange each class and pay attention to the growth of each individual, laying the foundation for students to acquire lifelong learning ability.

国际部全体教职工大会（2016.08.29）

The staff meeting of the International Department

中方教师和外国留学生合影（2018.04.09）

The photo of chinese teachers and exchange students

参加体育季活动的外籍教师（2018.10.12）

Foreign teachers participating in sports season activities

W 学 校 的 样 子
HAT THE SCHOOL LOOKS LIKE

富有特色的多样空间
Unique and Diverse Spaces

　　十一学校以学生的学习和成长为中心，打造了丰富的、现代化的学习环境：别具特色的学科教室、千兆校园网、开放式图书馆、一流的学生剧院、高端科学实验室、艺术排练厅、多功能体育馆、咖啡厅、空中花园、7个融汇中外美食的餐厅、舒适的学生公寓等，种种现代化设施与学习空间是学生的成长乐园和精神家园。

　　Centered on the students' learning and growth, BNDS has created modern and diversified learning environment: distinctive subject classrooms, gigabit campus network, open library, first-class student theater, high-end science laboratory, art rehearsal hall, multi-functional gymnasium, coffee shop, sky garden, seven restaurants offering Chinese and foreign cuisines, and comfortable student apartments, etc. All kinds of modern facilities and learning spaces are students' paradise for growth.

国际部阅览室（2016.12.26）

International Department Library

W 学 校 的 样 子
HAT THE SCHOOL LOOKS LIKE

学校操场（2018.06.29）

School Stadium

黑盒子剧场的演出（2018.12.19）

Performance in the Black Box Theater

WHAT THE SCHOOL LOOKS LIKE 学 校 的 样 子

放眼世界的文化日活动
Foreign Culture Day Activities

　　为了让学生感受不同国家的语言及地域文化，拓宽学生的视野，十一学校开设了以十多个国家名字命名的外国文化日活动，涵盖罗马尼亚、美国、英国、韩国、德国、法国、西班牙、加拿大、澳大利亚、巴西、俄罗斯、意大利等国家。文化日活动也是由学生来承办，包括美食文化、语言文化、文艺表演等内容，有时还会有相应国家的驻华大使参加，不同文化日活动的形式虽各不相同，却都充分体现了承办学生的心血汗水与聪明才智。

In order to let students experience the language and culture of different countries and broaden their horizons, BNDS has set up more than 10 Foreign Culture Days named after countries including Romania, the United States, the United Kingdom, South Korea, Germany, France, Spain, Canada, Australia, Brazil, Russia, Italy and others. Foreign Culture Day activities involving food culture, language culture and artistic performances are also organized by students. Sometimes ambassadors to China from foreign countries will also attend the events in person. Although activities varied on different foreign cultural days, they all reflect the hard work and ingenuity of students.

定期组织不同国家的文化日活动（2015.10.12）

Foreign Culture Day activity

W 学 校 的 样 子
HAT THE SCHOOL LOOKS LIKE

让我们一起跳舞（2019.11.21）

Let's dance

文化日活动结束后的创意合影（2014.11.20）
Creative group photo after the event

后　记

　　摄影犹如人的第三只眼，透过镜头，用方寸画幅就可呈现内容丰富的影像，特定情境下，可以说是一图胜千言。当我用镜头聚焦北京十一学校，我发现这所学校有许多值得按动快门的地方，有许多感人的场景和细节，有时还会有一些热闹非凡的活动，这一切都在与众不同地诠释着全新的教育。

　　我走进十一学校十年了，从校园里的一草一木到课堂上的老师学生，我非常熟悉和了解这所学校，我不断地用相机进行描述和记录。在十一学校的时间，我尝试用影像来解析这所学校的独特魅力，但这不是件容易的事情，因为十一学校的理念太多元、内涵太丰富。

　　十一学校走在教育改革的前沿，通过这些照片我们可以发现，十一学校的校园环境不一样、教育理念不一样、课程设计不一样、学科教室不一样、育人模式不一样、学生风貌不一样……这些不一样的特色正是这所学校的个性所在，也是这所学校的特别之处。透过镜头，我们看到学校与时俱进、不断变革，可谓新学校的榜样；我们也看到学生逐渐蜕变、脱颖而出，可谓青春激扬；我们还看到老师在这里辛勤耕耘、倍感幸福，可谓别具风采！通过解读十一学校的这些照片，我们能生动直观地看到当前教育改革的方向、步伐和成果。我想透过镜头里凝固的瞬间来描述，向人们展现这所学校不一样的内涵。

　　历经十年的时间，我在十一学校拍摄的照片已经不计其数，从几个移动硬盘里精心挑选了一百多幅汇编成册，希望能从不同的侧面来表现这所学校的某些特质。我想，将来再看这些图片，会更有历史价值，正如将来再看十一学校的这场改革一样。

在本书出版之际，我要感谢十一学校的广大师生，是他们的教育改革和实践让我深受感动，感谢他们配合我的拍摄工作；感谢李航老师对于书中文字的翻译，感谢在本书的选题策划、版式设计等环节给予帮助的老师和朋友们，感谢五洲传播出版社和源创图书给予的大力支持。

李 强

2022 年 6 月

Afterword

Photography is the third eye of a person. Through the lens, an image with rich connotations can be presented on a square-inch paper. Sometimes a picture is worth a thousand words. As I focus on Beijing National Day School with my lens, I find so many things worth a snapshot. There are touching scenes, moments and lively activities everywhere, all of which are distinctive in interpreting a fire-new education.

Having been working at BNDS for ten years, I am very familiar with the school, from every grass and tree on campus to teachers and students in classrooms. And I keep describing and recording it with my camera. During my time at BNDS, I've been trying to analyze the unique glamour of this school through images, but it is not an easy task, for the school's education philosophy is so diverse and rich in connotations.

BNDS is at the forefront of educational reform. Through the photos we can find how the school is different, from the campus environment, educational philosophy, and curriculum design, to subject classrooms and student features. These distinctive characteristics are what make the school unique and extraordinary. Through BNDS with the lens, the school changs with the times and sets an example of an innovative school, the students grow, stand out, and show their youthful vigor, the teachers dedicate and fulfill themselves with love and happiness. By interpreting these vivid photos, the direction, pace and results of current educational reform were completely revealed. Through the captured moments, I hope to display the unique features of this school.

After taking countless photos at BNDS in the past decade, I carefully selected over a hundred of them to compile this book, with the hope to show special qualities of this school from different perspectives. I believe the pictures will be more historically valuable in the future, just as it will be valuable to look at the educational reform at BNDS in retrospect.

On the occasion of the publication of this book, I would like to express my greatest gratitude to teachers and students at BNDS, whose educational reform and practices touched me deeply, Ms. Li Hang for the translation of the book. Thanks to teachers and friends who offered significant help for the production of this book. I would also like to thank China Intercontinental Press and Yuanchuang Press for their generous support.

Li Qiang
June, 2022